THE
ONE-DISH
BIBLE

pi

Publications International, Ltd.

Pictured on the front cover *(left to right):* Meatballs in Burgundy Sauce *(page 26)* and Greek-Style Chicken *(page 92).*
Pictured on the back cover: Lickety-Split Paella Pronto *(page 292).*

ISBN-13: 978-1-4508-6313-1
ISBN-10: 1-4508-6313-2

Manufactured in China.

8 7 6 5 4 3 2 1

Microwave Cooking: Microwave ovens vary in wattage. Use the cooking times as guidelines and check for doneness before adding more time.

Preparation/Cooking Times: Preparation times are based on the approximate amount of time required to assemble the recipe before cooking, baking, chilling or serving. These times include preparation steps such as measuring, chopping and mixing. The fact that some preparations and cooking can be done simultaneously is taken into account. Preparation of optional ingredients and serving suggestions is not included.

Publications International, Ltd.

contents

Overview

If you find yourself asking "what exactly are one-dish meals?" believe it or not, you probably already have a good idea. Essentially, one-dish meals are prepared in one dish. While soups, stews and some stir-fries also fit this loose definition, they may or may not be complete meals. One-dish meals usually include meat, vegetables and starches such as pasta or potatoes, prepared in a single cooking utensil. The three basic types of one-dish recipes are casseroles, skillet meals and slow cooker meals. Each one is incredibly convenient for home cooks and offers a memorable blend of flavors for family-pleasing meals.

While many casseroles feature just a starch and a meat, others are complete meals with vegetables. This eliminates having to coordinate the cooking of vegetable side dishes. Another added benefit is that leftover one-dish casseroles are just as delicious to eat as they are easy to reheat and clean up.

Over the years, one-dish meals have evolved from a rough concept to a more refined technique with casseroles and skillet meals predating the slow cooker by centuries. The word "casserole" dates back to the ancient Greek and Roman languages. Crude metal pots in use as early as the seventh century were the predecessor of the modern skillet.

One-dish meals, particularly casseroles, initially became popular cooking methods out of necessity. Most every culture's history includes lean periods when meat was scarce. For that reason, many people became skilled at making small amounts of meat stretch to feed many mouths. Casseroles were the perfect solution—an entire meal in one container. Some early examples of "casserole" dishes include Italian lasagna, Spanish paella, and Irish shepherd's pie.

Eventually, necessity gave way to busier times. Home cooks needed to make meal preparation easier and faster to fit their busy schedules. Skillet meals were the answer. Using their skillets to cook entire meals saved both time and energy.

Finally, technological innovation drove the invention of a new kind of one-dish meal preparation, the slow cooker. Introduced in the 1970s, this revolutionary kitchen appliance had an immediate impact on how meals were prepared. Ingredients could be assembled in minutes and cooked unattended for hours. Suddenly home cooks were freed from their kitchens.

In our modern and fast-paced world, these one-dish meals have found new life. It's not merely a case of history repeating itself, rather it's more like history being applied to the present.

The Casserole

The first known casserole recipe was published in England around 1705. Ever since then, nothing can really match a bubbling casserole fresh from the oven. Cooking for parties or just weekday family meals, the convenience of preparing a casserole takes the stress out of meal preparation and makes cleanup easy. The warm comfort of casserole cooking extends far beyond satisfying appetites; it also leaves a lasting impression in everyone's hearts and memories.

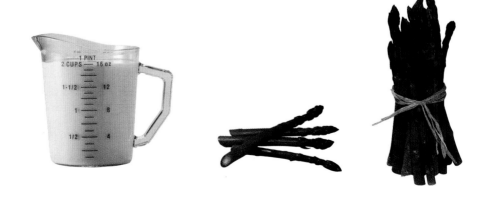

Determining Dish Size

Considering the vast array of casseroles and baking dishes available, it might seem like a daunting task to select the right casserole dish. It's really not that difficult. Most casseroles and baking dishes list their measurements on the bottom; for those that do not, the sizes can be easily measured.

For either rectangular or square casserole dishes, just measure the dimensions from one inside edge to the opposite inside edge (for both length and width), then measure the inside depth, top to bottom. Round and oval casseroles are measured by volume and their capacity is listed by the number of quarts they will hold.

To determine capacity, fill a measuring cup, pour its contents into the casserole and repeat until the casserole is full, keeping track of how many cups have been used.

Casserole Dish Substitution Guide

Casserole Capacity	Baking Dish Size	Cups
1 quart	8-inch pie plate	4
1½ quarts	8×8×1½-inch	6
	11×7-inch	
2 quarts	8×8×2-inch	8
	9×9×1½-inch	
	9-inch deep-dish	
2½ quarts	9×9×2-inch	10
3½ to 4 quarts	13×9-inch	14 to 16

Tips & Techniques

Sometimes success is measured in the small things that go into making a dish. Lining a casserole dish with foil, for example, can often make cleanup easier. Some additional tips, techniques, time-savers and others helpful hints include:

- Pasta and rice should be slightly undercooked until almost tender but still chewy. The pasta or rice will continue to cook during baking.

- Occasionally casserole recipes suggest browning meat and poultry. The two most common methods are sautéing and roasting.

- When sautéing small pieces, make sure the food to be cooked is cut into uniform shapes and is dry. If unevenly cut, the food will not cook at the same rate. And any excess liquid might cause dangerous splatters and cause food to steam rather than brown.

- When recipes call for cooked meat or poultry a good technique to use is poaching. Add just enough liquid to cover the food and gently simmer over a very low flame until the meat or poultry is juicy and tender. Do not boil the liquid or the meat will become tough.

- Casseroles can be prepared in advance and frozen unbaked until you need them. Line the casserole dish with plastic wrap, folding the edges over. Then spray with nonstick cooking spray; add all the combined casserole ingredients in the lined dish and freeze. As soon as the casserole is frozen, lift it out of the dish by the edges of the plastic wrap and place in an airtight, resealable plastic freezer bag. Just keep it in the freezer until you're ready to eat it.

- To cook a frozen casserole, simply remove it from the freezer, discarding all plastic wrap and place it into a casserole dish. Defrost in the refrigerator and bake in a preheated oven as the recipe directs.

- For some frozen casseroles, thawing is not required; they can go straight from the freezer to the oven. Usually this means doubling the baking time and checking for doneness about 15 minutes prior to the final cooking time.

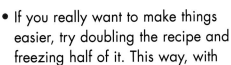

- If you really want to make things easier, try doubling the recipe and freezing half of it. This way, with minimal additional effort, you've prepared two meals in the time it takes for one.

Whatever your preference, there is a casserole recipe for you. Discover warm and satisfying meals that are easy to prepare and don't make a mess of your kitchen. Casseroles are the timely answer to cooking homemade, comforting meals that fit into your busy lifestyle.

The Pantry

Having a well-stocked pantry can really make preparing casseroles a snap. Some products to keep readily available include:

Basic Pantry

Dry Goods
- Biscuit mix
- Bread crumbs
- Cereals
- Dried and canned beans
- Flour
- Nuts
- Pasta
- Rice (white, brown and/or wild)
- Stuffing mix

Canned and Jarred Goods
- Broth, bouillon
- Canned milk
- Condensed soup
- Oils
- Pasta sauces
- Tomatoes, tomato sauce
- Tuna, chicken, salmon, ham
- Vinegars

Time-Saving Pantry

Refrigerated Products
- Prepared polenta
- Cooked chicken strips
- Fresh pasta
- Prepared doughs

Frozen Products
- Frozen potatoes, vegetables
- Frozen pastry, phyllo dough
- Frozen tortellini, pierogi

Shelf-stable Products
- Canned beans: kidney, black, chickpeas, chili beans
- Canned diced tomatoes with chilies and seasonings
- Canned broths
- Ketchups, salsas, pestos, barbecue sauces
- Marinades, salad dressings
- Quick bread mixes
- Stuffing mixes

Ground Meats

Ground meats are some of the most important ingredients in one-dish meals. While these versatile meats can be used in a variety of ways in recipes, in skillet dishes they are browned, defatted, then combined with other ingredients. It seems simple enough, but here are some tips to make preparation of ground meats even better:

- When browning ground meat, break it up into ¾- to 1-inch pieces. The larger pieces will give the dish better flavor. Smaller crumbles will get dry and retain less flavor.

- Cooking ground meat with dried seasonings adds more flavor to the finished dish than adding the seasoning to the sauce. Dried seasonings tend to release their flavors when heated over direct heat.

- For quicker thawing, freeze fresh ground meats in small packages or patties. To properly thaw frozen meats, place them in the refrigerator overnight or thaw in the microwave oven before cooking. Always immediately use meat thawed in a microwave oven.

- To brown 1 pound of ground meat using your microwave, place it in a microwavable colander and set it, in a deep microwavable bowl. Heat at HIGH 4 to 5 minutes or until the meat is no longer pink, stirring twice during cooking. Discard the grease which accumulates in the bowl.

- To meet USDA standards, all ground beef must be at least 70 percent lean. Ground sirloin and ground round are the leanest. Ground chuck contains more fat and therefore produces juicier hamburgers and meat loaf.

Toppings

Casseroles usually feature a delicious combination of textures, from creamy to crispy, and the toppings are the finishing touches. While crispy toppings jazz up a casserole, melted cheese helps to seal in flavors. Some toppings to choose from typically include:

- **Homemade breadcrumbs or croutons:** they add a crispy texture-and they're a great way to utilize leftover bread.

- **Toasted almonds:** they add a wonderful rich nutty flavor to most any casserole.

- **Fruits or vegetables:** chopped bell peppers, carrots or dried cranberries add a splash of color.

- **Cheese:** it can range from gooey melted cheese to slightly crispy depending on length of cooking time.

- **Crushed Chips:** These add a salty and crispy crunch to casseroles and are a great way to put to use the crumbled bits that always seem to end up at the bottom of the chip bag.

- **Mashed Potatoes:** Either leftover or instant mashed potatoes can give most any casserole a delicious lid with a warm and soft inside.

Featured toppings might involve one specific choice or a combination of options. It's a good opportunity to unleash your creativity. For instance, unsweetened cereals can be crushed, broken into bite-sized pieces or left whole to add a special texture to casserole toppings.

The Skillet

Having made a name for themselves in the wild American west of the late 1800's, skillets have long been a trusted tool for cooks, never more so than when cooking an entire meal for a lot of hungry people. An entire meal in one skillet? Although it might sound like an amazing feat, it is quite possible as well as practical. Skillet meals are easy to prepare and very tasty. Typically, there are usually four components in a skillet meal: a protein source, vegetables, sauce and either pasta, rice or a grain. When it comes right down to it, skillet meals are a great way to use up a variety of leftover foods or just a simple alternative to everyday cooking.

Skillet meals are also versatile. While there are many recipes for skillet meals in this book, there always remains the option of creatively customizing these meals to suit your family's tastes. When cooking for a low-fat diet, for instance, ground turkey easily replaces ground beef. And if no one likes zucchini, replace it with green beans or bell peppers.

The sky is the limit with the many combinations that are possible. If you use about 1 pound of meat, 2 cups of liquid, 1 cup of uncooked starch and 2 cups of vegetables (whether fresh, frozen or pre-cooked), you should have approximately the right amounts of everything. The following chart shows how you can mix and match ingredients to create your own special skillet meals. Just choose one ingredient from each column.

Skillet Meals Mix and Match

Meat	Vegetable	Sauce	Starch
Beef	Frozen vegetables	Cream soups	Rice, uncooked
Chicken	Corn	Pasta sauces	Macaroni, cooked
Pork	Carrots	Beef broth	Hash brown potatoes, frozen
Shrimp	Beans	Tomato soups	Bow tie pasta, uncooked
Ham	Bell peppers	Chicken broth	Couscous

Choosing a Skillet

There are very few hard and fast rules when it comes to equipment selection. But if you're in the market for a new skillet or just want to replace an old one, look for one that is heavy, conducts heat evenly, has a tight-fitting cover and a sturdy handle. Skillets with either straight or slightly sloping sides will work well. Skillets come in sizes from 6 to 14 inches in diameter. Most skillet meals for four require a 12-inch skillet. A second, short handle opposite the long handle is a convenient option with 12-inch or larger skillets.

Copper is often considered the most efficient material at conducting heat.

However, copper skillets and pans are also very expensive and require more care to keep clean. Aluminum pans or stainless steel pans with cores or bottoms of aluminum or copper are sensible options with little performance loss. There is also a wide variety of nonstick coated pans which offer good heat conductivity but require specific care for cleaning.

Choosing between nonstick surfaces or noncoated pans is really up to the individual.

Personal preference often plays a significant role in what each cook will decide. The important thing is to find out what works best for you.

Tips & Techniques

A well-stocked pantry and freezer and the right-sized skillet go a long way to making meal planning easier. It might also be helpful to keep the following in mind:

- Leftovers, like cooked pasta and rice, meat and poultry, and vegetables, cut cooking time in half.

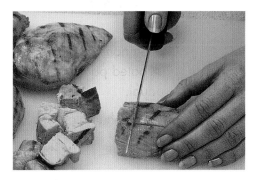

- Ingredients that are cut into similarly-sized pieces will cook more evenly.

- Keep stirring! Occasionally stir the food during cooking so that nothing sticks to the bottom of the skillet.

- For those stubborn, sticky foods that just won't come clean just remove the skillet meal and heat the pan slightly.

- Slowly pour enough hot water to cover the bottom of the pan, then scrape with a wooden spoon. Those stuck-on bits will come right off.

Expand your cooking horizons with skillet meals. The skillet has left its mark on modern cooking and now provides a versatile, time-saving option for cooking entire meals. Skillet meals are a convenient one-dish meal option that anyone can perfect.

The Slow Cooker

The Slow Cooker

While a bevy of specialty appliances have made their way through kitchens over the years, one of the most useful inventions was the slow cooker. Not since the microwave introduced its unique method of heating food has a kitchen appliance had this dramatic of an effect on how entire meals are prepared.

Perfectly filling a niche in today's fast-paced culture where families barely have time to fit dinner in between school, work and soccer practice, much less cook entire meals, the slow cooker was welcomed as a savior. Suddenly meals could be prepared in advance, placed in a slow cooker before setting off for work, and then cooked unsupervised all day. People could come home to ready-to-eat full meals. This afforded more leisure time while also reducing clean-up time. Plus the slow cooker can act as an extra "burner" for entertaining or holiday cooking. And on those hot summer days, it will also keep your kitchen cool since you won't have to turn on the oven.

The most common slow cooker models have a crockery insert, heat coils either circling the crockery insert or embedded into the base, and two settings of LOW or HIGH. The LOW temperature setting is approximately 200°F and the HIGH setting is about 300°F. One hour on HIGH equals 2 to 2½ hours on LOW. Some models also have adjustable thermostats, but most slow cooker recipes are written with the LOW/HIGH temperature control in mind. Another added benefit is that slow cookers can help save money on electrical bills since they use less energy on the LOW setting than most light bulbs.

Adapting Conventional Recipes

Most recipes that are not specifically written for slow cookers can be adapted to be cooked in one. If possible, find a similar recipe that is written for a slow cooker. Consider reducing the amount of liquid (sometimes by as much as half). Meals prepared in a slow cooker tend to retain a considerable amount of moisture as compared to conventional cooking methods where evaporation is expected to occur.

Cooking Guidelines

For converting conventional cooking times to slow cooker times, use the following as a guide:

Conventional Recipe	Cook on LOW	Cook on HIGH
30 to 45 minutes	6 to 10 hours	3 to 4 hours
50 minutes to 3 hours	8 to 15 hours	4 to 6 hours

Tips & Techniques

When cooking a meal in a slow cooker, whether from a recipe specifically written for a slow cooker or one that has been adapted, it is imperative to keep the lid on the slow cooker. Some slow cooker recipes call for stirring but typically only near the end of the cooking cycle. Removing the lid during cooking when it is not called for can add as much as twenty minutes per each time the lid is lifted.

The meats used in slow cookers are an important consideration. Slow cookers can cook most any type of food, from soups and stews to party snacks and desserts. For meat dishes, less tender and less expensive cuts of meat are a good choice. The extended slower cooking times will help tenderize meat. Visible fat should be trimmed off before cooking meats in a slow cooker. Cuts where the fat is less visible (ground meats, ribs, etc.) should be browned and drained before adding to the slow cooker as this will help to reduce excess fat. Browning some meats and poultry ahead of time will add flavor and color to some dishes. With poultry, use skinless cuts or remove the skin prior to cooking.

As with meats, special attention should be given to vegetables cooked in slow cookers. Not every vegetable cooks at the same rate. Potatoes, carrots and other root vegetables are more fibrous or thicker; they can take longer to cook than most other vegetables and often longer than meats. These types of vegetables should be cut into small, uniform pieces and placed closer to the bottom of the slow cooker. If using frozen vegetables, make sure to thaw them ahead of time to prevent and adding unnecessary additional moisture and cooking time.

Despite your best efforts to reduce the amount of fat on meats and to prevent additional moisture from frozen vegetables, your slow cooked meal might not turn out as thick as you like it or it might have too much fat in it. Try any of the following tips to address these problems:

To thicken a meal at the end of cooking time, remove solid foods with a slotted spoon, make a smooth paste of ¼ cup each flour and water (or 2 tablespoons each cornstarch and water) and stir into cooking liquid. Turn the slow cooker to HIGH and cook about 15 minutes until mixture boils and liquid thickens.

The next time you prepare the recipe, add quick-cooking tapioca at the beginning of the cook time to thicken while the dish cooks.

To remove fat from juices, remove the solids foods with a slotted spoon and let the liquid stand about 5 minutes. The fat will rise to the surface and you can skim it off with a large spoon.

Some recipes call for using foil handles to lift a dish or a meatloaf out of the slow cooker. Foil handles are easy to make; just follow these easy directions.

Tear off three 18×3-inch strips of heavy-duty foil. Crisscross the strips so they resemble spokes of a wheel. Place your dish or food in the center of the strips.

Pull foil strips up and over, and place into the slow cooker. Leave them in while you cook so you can easily lift the item out again when it is ready.

Food Safety and Handling

One of the most important aspects of food preparation, remains practicing proper food safety. Some basics to keep in mind include:

- Cover and refrigerate food prepared in advance, including ingredients and whole recipes. Store uncooked meats and vegetables separately.

- Do not reheat foods in a slow cooker, even if they've been initially prepared in one.

- Do not use the slow cooker to defrost and cook frozen foods. It's best to defrost foods slowly in a refrigerator or, if you're in more of a hurry, to use your microwave's defrost setting.

- Remove the finished dish from the slow cooker when you've turned the heat off. Do not leave food in a slow cooker very long after cooking.

Ingredients

Recipes often call for ingredients that sometimes you may not have available or which might be difficult to find. While it's best to follow recipes closely, the following substitutions will work just as well.

Ingredient Substitution Guide

Ingredient	Substitution
If you don't have:	*Use:*
Basic ingredients	
2½ tablespoons flour	Arrowroot (1 tablespoon)
Baking powder (1 teaspoon)	¼ teaspoon baking soda plus ½ teaspoon cream of tartar
Bread crumbs (1 cup)	1 cup cracker crumbs or matzo meal
Broth, chicken or beef (1 cup)	1 bouillon cube or ½ teaspoon granules mixed with 1 cup boiling water
Butter (1 cup or 2 sticks)	1 cup margarine or ⅞ cup vegetable oil
Cheddar cheese (1 cup shredded)	1 cup shredded Colby or Monterey Jack cheese
Cornstarch (1 tablespoon)	2 tablespoons all-purpose flour or 2 teaspoons arrowroot
Cottage cheese (1 cup)	1 cup farmer's cheese or ricotta cheese
Cream cheese (1 cup)	1 cup puréed cottage cheese or 1 cup plain yogurt, strained overnight in cheesecloth
Cream, half-and-half (1 cup)	1½ tablespoons melted butter plus enough whole milk to equal 1 cup
Cream, whipping or heavy cream (1 cup)	1 cup evaporated milk or ¾ cup milk (1 cup) plus ⅓ cup butter
Cream, whipping cream, whipped (1 cup)	2 cups whipped dessert topping
Egg (1 whole)	2 egg yolks plus 1 tablespoon cold water
Garlic (1 small clove)	⅛ teaspoon garlic powder or ¼ teaspoon garlic salt

Ingredient Substitution Guide

Ingredient	Substitution
If you don't have:	**Use:**
Basic ingredients	
Ketchup (1 cup)	1 cup tomato sauce plus 1 teaspoon vinegar plus 1 tablespoon sugar
Lemon juice (1 teaspoon)	½ teaspoon vinegar, lime juice or white wine
Lemon or orange peel, fresh (1 teaspoon)	½ teaspoon dried peel
Mayonnaise (1 cup)	1 cup sour cream or yogurt
Milk, evaporated (1 cup)	1 cup light cream
Mushrooms, fresh (½ pound)	1 can (4 ounces) mushrooms
Mustard, prepared (1 tablespoon)	1 teaspoon powdered mustard
Onions, minced (¼ cup)	1 tablespoon dry minced onion
Parmesan cheese, grated (½ cup)	½ cup grated Asiago or Romano cheese
Raisins (1 cup)	1 cup dried currants or dried cranberries
Saffron (½ teaspoon)	½ teaspoon turmeric
Sour cream (1 cup)	1 cup plain yogurt
Soy sauce (½ cup)	¼ cup Worcestershire sauce mixed with ¼ cup water
Tomato juice (1 cup)	½ cup tomato sauce plus ½ cup water
Tomato sauce (1 cup)	⅜ cup tomato paste plus ½ cup water
Vinegar (1 teaspoon)	2 teaspoons lemon or lime juice
Wine (1 cup)	1 cup chicken or beef broth or 1 cup fruit juice mixed with 2 teaspoons vinegar

Herbs are the aromatic leaves of herbaceous plants (plants with stems that are soft rather than woody). They are valued in the kitchen for their natural aromatic oils, which are used to accent and enhance the flavor of foods or, on occasion, to provide the essential ingredient in a recipe.

Spices come from the seeds, bark, roots, fruit or flowers of plants. They add flavor and color to both sweet and savory dishes. For thousands of years, spices were an important world commodity, actively traded and in part responsible for expeditions that led to the discovery of the New World.

Fresh herbs for cooking have enjoyed a surge in popularity in recent years. Some of the more common fresh herbs, such as basil, chives, dill and oregano, are available year-round. Dried herbs and spices, both leaf and ground form, are readily available all year in any supermarket. Purchase fresh herbs in small quantities as they can be very perishable. Store them for the short-term by placing the stems in water. Cover leaves loosely with a plastic bag and store in the refrigerator. Fresh herbs stored this way should last between two to five days.

There are many herb-and-spice blends available at supermarkets. Most are composed of spices and herbs found in the spice section of grocery stores and they have the advantage of convenience.

Herbs and Spices Substitution Guide

Ingredient	Substitution
If you don't have:	*Use:*
Herbs and Spices	
Allspice (1 teaspoon)	½ teaspoon ground cinnamon, ¼ teaspoon ground ginger and ¼ teaspoon ground cloves
Ginger, ground (1 teaspoon)	2 teaspoons finely chopped fresh ginger
Herbs, dried (1 teaspoon)	1 tablespoon chopped fresh herbs
Poultry seasoning (1 teaspoon)	¾ teaspoon dried sage plus ¼ teaspoon dried thyme or dried marjoram

Bountiful Beef

Meatballs in Burgundy Sauce

60 frozen prepared fully-cooked meatballs
3 cups chopped onions
1½ cups water
1 cup red wine
2 packages (about 1 ounce each) beef gravy mix
¼ cup ketchup
1 tablespoon dried oregano leaves
1 package (8 ounces) egg noodles

Slow Cooker Directions

1. Combine meatballs, onions, water, wine, gravy mix, ketchup and oregano in slow cooker; stir to blend.

2. Cover; cook on HIGH 5 hours.

3. Meanwhile cook noodles according to package directions. Serve meatballs with noodles. *Makes 6 to 8 servings*

Serving Suggestion: Serve as an appetizer with cocktail toothpicks and remaining sauce as a dip.

Meatballs in Burgundy Sauce

Tamale Beef Squares

1 (6½-ounce) package corn muffin and cornbread mix
⅓ cup fat-free (skim) milk
¼ cup cholesterol-free egg substitute
1 tablespoon canola oil
1 pound 90% lean ground beef
¾ cup chopped onion
1 cup frozen corn kernels
1 (14½-ounce) can Mexican-style stewed tomatoes, undrained
2 teaspoons cornstarch
¾ cup (3 ounces) shredded reduced-fat sharp Cheddar cheese

1. Preheat oven to 400°F. Spray 12×8-inch baking dish with nonstick cooking spray.

2. Stir together corn muffin mix, milk, egg substitute and oil. Spread in bottom of prepared dish.

3. Cook ground beef and onion in large skillet over medium-high heat until beef is lightly browned, stirring to break up meat; drain fat. Stir in corn.

4. Mix together undrained tomatoes and cornstarch, breaking up any large pieces of tomato. Stir into beef mixture. Bring to a boil, stirring frequently.

5. Spoon beef mixture over cornbread mixture. Cover with foil. Bake 15 minutes. Uncover; bake 10 minutes more. Sprinkle with cheese. Return to oven; bake 2 to 3 minutes or until cheese melts. Let stand 5 minutes. Cut into squares.

Makes 6 servings

Tamale Beef Squares

Beef & Broccoli Pepper Steak

3 tablespoons margarine or butter, divided
1 pound sirloin or top round steak, cut into thin strips
1 (6.8-ounce) package RICE-A-RONI® Beef Flavor
2 cups broccoli flowerets
½ cup red or green bell pepper strips
1 small onion, thinly sliced

1. In large skillet over medium-high heat, melt 1 tablespoon margarine. Add steak; sauté 3 minutes or until just browned. Remove from skillet; set aside.

2. In same skillet over medium heat, sauté rice-vermicelli mix with remaining 2 tablespoons margarine until vermicelli is golden brown. Slowly stir in 2½ cups water and Special Seasonings; bring to a boil. Reduce heat to low. Cover; simmer 10 minutes.

3. Stir in steak, broccoli, bell pepper and onion; return to a simmer. Cover; simmer 5 to 10 minutes or until rice is tender. *Makes 4 servings*

Prep Time: 10 minutes
Cook Time: 30 minutes

Beef & Broccoli Pepper Steak

Shepherd's Pie

1⅓ cups instant mashed potato buds
1⅔ cups milk
  2 tablespoons margarine or butter
  1 teaspoon salt, divided
  1 pound ground beef
¼ teaspoon black pepper
  1 jar (12 ounces) beef gravy
  1 package (10 ounces) frozen mixed vegetables, thawed and
     drained
¾ cup grated Parmesan cheese

1. Preheat broiler. Prepare 4 servings of mashed potatoes according to package directions using milk, margarine and ½ teaspoon salt.

2. While mashed potatoes are cooking, brown meat in medium broilerproof skillet over medium-high heat, stirring to separate meat. Drain drippings. Sprinkle meat with remaining ½ teaspoon salt and pepper. Add gravy and vegetables; mix well. Cook over medium-low heat 5 minutes or until hot.

3. Spoon prepared potatoes around outside edge of skillet, leaving 3-inch circle in center. Sprinkle cheese evenly over potatoes. Broil 4 to 5 inches from heat 3 minutes or until cheese is golden brown and meat mixture is bubbly. *Makes 4 servings*

Prep and Cook Time: 28 minutes

Swiss Steak

1 onion, sliced into thick rings
1 clove garlic, minced
1 beef round steak (about 2 pounds), cut into 8 pieces
  All-purpose flour
  Salt
  Black pepper
1 can (28 ounces) whole tomatoes, undrained
1 can (10¾ ounces) condensed tomato soup, undiluted
3 medium unpeeled potatoes, diced
1 package (16 ounces) frozen peas and carrots
1 cup sliced celery
  Additional vegetables

Slow Cooker Directions

1. Place onion and garlic in slow cooker.

2. Dredge steak in flour seasoned with salt and pepper. Shake off excess flour. Place steak in slow cooker. Add tomatoes with juice. Cover with tomato soup. Add potatoes, peas and carrots, celery and any additional vegetables.

3. Cover; cook on HIGH 4 to 6 hours or until meat and potatoes are tender.

Makes 8 servings

Fiery Chili Beef

1 beef flank steak (1 to 1½ pounds)
1 can (28 ounces) diced tomatoes, undrained
1 can (15 ounces) pinto beans, rinsed and drained
1 medium onion, chopped
2 cloves garlic, minced
½ teaspoon salt
½ teaspoon ground cumin
¼ teaspoon black pepper
1 chipotle chile pepper canned in adobo sauce
1 teaspoon adobo sauce from canned chipotle chile pepper
Flour tortillas

Slow Cooker Directions

1. Cut flank steak in 6 evenly-sized pieces. Place flank steak, tomatoes with juice, beans, onion, garlic, salt, cumin and black pepper into slow cooker.

2. Dice chile pepper. Add pepper and adobo sauce to slow cooker; mix well.

3. Cover; cook on LOW 7 to 8 hours. Serve with tortillas.   *Makes 6 servings*

Tip: Chipotle chile peppers are dried, smoked jalapeño peppers with a very hot yet smoky, sweet flavor. They can be found dried, pickled and canned in adobo sauce.

Prep Time: 15 minutes
Cook Time: 7 to 8 hours

Fiery Chili Beef

Red Cloud Beef and Onions

2¼ cups nonfat milk
1½ cups water
1½ cups yellow cornmeal
½ cup grated Parmesan cheese
1 tablespoon butter or margarine
4 medium yellow onions, sliced (1 pound 6 ounces)
2 teaspoons vegetable oil
1 pound lean ground beef or pork
2 to 3 teaspoons chili powder (or to taste)
½ cup canned whole pimientos or roasted red bell peppers,
  cut into ½-inch strips
2 cans (4 ounces each) whole green chilies, cut into ½-inch strips

For cornmeal base, combine milk, water and cornmeal in saucepan. Place over medium heat and cook, stirring, until mixture bubbles. Continue cooking 30 to 60 seconds or until mixture is consistency of soft mashed potatoes. Remove from heat; stir in cheese and butter. Spoon into 2½-quart casserole. Sauté onions in oil in large skillet until soft. Spoon into casserole in ring around edge. In same skillet, sauté beef or pork until browned; stir in chili powder. Spoon meat mixture into center of casserole. Arrange pimientos and chilies in latticework pattern over top. Cover and bake at 400°F for 25 to 30 minutes or until hot in center. Serve with dollops of sour cream, if desired. *Makes 6 servings*

Favorite recipe from **National Onion Association**

Red Cloud Beef and Onions

Spicy Italian Beef

1 boneless beef chuck roast (3 to 4 pounds)
1 jar (12 ounces) peperoncini
1 can (14½ ounces) beef broth
1 can (12 ounces) beer
1 package (1 ounce) Italian salad dressing mix
1 loaf French bread, cut into thick slices
10 slices provolone cheese (optional)

Slow Cooker Directions

1. Trim fat from roast. Cut roast, if necessary, to fit in slow cooker, leaving meat in as many large pieces as possible.

2. Drain peperoncini; pull off stem ends and discard. Add peperoncini, broth, beer and salad dressing mix to slow cooker; *do not stir.* Cover; cook on LOW 8 to 10 hours.

3. Remove meat from slow cooker; shred with 2 forks. Return shredded meat to slow cooker; mix well.

4. Serve on French bread, topped with cheese, if desired. Add additional sauce and peperoncini, if desired. *Makes 8 to 10 servings*

Tip: Peperoncini are thin, 2- to 3-inch-long mild pickled peppers. Look for them in the Italian foods or pickled foods section of the grocery store.

Spicy Italian Beef

Beef and Vegetables in Rich Burgundy Sauce

1 package (8 ounces) sliced mushrooms
1 package (8 ounces) baby carrots
1 medium green bell pepper, cut into thin strips
1 boneless beef chuck roast (2½ pounds)
1 can (10½ ounces) condensed golden mushroom soup, undiluted
¼ cup dry red wine or beef broth
1 tablespoon Worcestershire sauce
1 package (1 ounce) dry onion soup mix
¼ teaspoon black pepper
3 tablespoons cornstarch
2 tablespoons water
4 cups hot cooked noodles
Chopped fresh parsley (optional)

Slow Cooker Directions

1. Place mushrooms, carrots and bell pepper in slow cooker. Place roast on top of vegetables. Combine mushroom soup, wine, Worcestershire sauce, soup mix and black pepper in medium bowl; mix well. Pour soup mixture over roast. Cover; cook on LOW 8 to 10 hours.

2. Transfer roast to cutting board; cover with foil. Let stand 10 to 15 minutes before slicing.

3. Blend cornstarch and water until smooth. Turn slow cooker to HIGH. Stir cornstarch mixture into vegetable mixture; cook 10 minutes or until thickened. Serve beef and vegetables with sauce over cooked noodles. Garnish with parsley, if desired.   *Makes 6 to 8 servings*

Sauerbraten

1 boneless beef rump roast (1¼ pounds)
3 cups baby carrots
1½ cups fresh or frozen pearl onions
¼ cup raisins
½ cup water
½ cup red wine vinegar
1 tablespoon honey
½ teaspoon salt
½ teaspoon dry mustard
½ teaspoon garlic-pepper seasoning
¼ teaspoon ground cloves
¼ cup crushed crisp gingersnap cookies (5 cookies)

Slow Cooker Directions

1. Heat large nonstick skillet over medium heat until hot. Brown roast on all sides. Place roast, carrots, onions and raisins in slow cooker.

2. Combine water, vinegar, honey, salt, mustard, garlic-pepper seasoning and cloves in large bowl; mix well. Pour mixture over meat and vegetables. Cover; cook on LOW 4 to 6 hours or until internal temperature reaches 145°F when tested with meat thermometer inserted into thickest part of roast.

3. Transfer roast to cutting board; cover with foil. Let stand 10 to 15 minutes before slicing. Internal temperature will continue to rise 5°F to 10°F during stand time.

4. Remove vegetables with slotted spoon to bowl; cover to keep warm. Stir crushed cookies into sauce mixture in slow cooker. Cover; cook on HIGH 10 to 15 minutes or until sauce thickens. Serve meat and vegetables with sauce.   *Makes 5 servings*

Pizza Pie Meatloaf

2 pounds ground beef
1½ cups shredded mozzarella cheese, divided
½ cup unseasoned dry breadcrumbs
1 cup tomato sauce, divided
¼ cup grated Parmesan cheese
¼ cup *French's*® Worcestershire Sauce
1 tablespoon dried oregano leaves
1⅓ cups *French's*® French Fried Onions

1. Preheat oven to 350°F. Combine beef, *½ cup* mozzarella, bread crumbs, *½ cup* tomato sauce, Parmesan cheese, Worcestershire and oregano in large bowl; stir with fork until well blended.

2. Place meat mixture into round pizza pan with edge or pie plate and shape into 9×1-inch round. Bake 35 minutes or until no longer pink in center and internal temperature reads 160°F. Drain fat.

3. Top with remaining mozzarella cheese, tomato sauce and French Fried Onions. Bake 5 minutes or until cheese is melted and onions are golden. Cut into wedges to serve. *Makes 6 to 8 servings*

Prep Time: 10 minutes
Cook Time: 40 minutes

Pizza Pie Meatloaf

Chili & Potato Casserole

1 pound HILLSHIRE FARM® Yard-O-Beef, cut into small cubes
1 cup chopped yellow onion
1 egg, lightly beaten
¼ cup bread crumbs
1 tablespoon chili powder
   Salt to taste
3 cups prepared mashed potatoes
1 can (11 ounces) succotash, drained
¼ cup thinly sliced green onions
1 cup (4 ounces) shredded taco-flavored cheese

Preheat oven to 375°F.

Combine Yard-O-Beef, yellow onion, egg, bread crumbs, chili powder and salt in large bowl; mix thoroughly. Pour beef mixture into medium baking dish, pressing mixture firmly onto bottom of dish. Bake 20 minutes. Pour off any juices.

Mix potatoes, succotash and green onions in medium bowl. Spread potato mixture over beef mixture; sprinkle top with cheese. Broil 3 to 4 inches from heat source 3 to 5 minutes or until top is lightly browned. *Makes 4 to 6 servings*

Farm Fresh Tip: Frozen casseroles should be reheated in a 350°F oven. Add some liquid during cooking if the food seems dry.

Chili & Potato Casserole

Chuckwagon BBQ Rice Round-Up

1 pound lean ground beef
1 (6.8-ounce) package RICE-A-RONI® Beef Flavor
2 tablespoons margarine or butter
2 cups frozen corn
½ cup prepared barbecue sauce
½ cup (2 ounces) shredded Cheddar cheese

1. In large skillet over medium-high heat, brown ground beef until well cooked. Remove from skillet; drain. Set aside.

2. In same skillet over medium heat, sauté rice-vermicelli mix with margarine until vermicelli is golden brown.

3. Slowly stir in 2½ cups water, corn and Special Seasonings; bring to a boil. Reduce heat to low. Cover; simmer 15 to 20 minutes or until rice is tender.

4. Stir in barbecue sauce and ground beef. Sprinkle with cheese. Cover; let stand 3 to 5 minutes or until cheese is melted. *Makes 4 servings*

Tip: Salsa can be substituted for barbecue sauce.

Prep Time: 5 minutes
Cook Time: 25 minutes

Chuckwagon BBQ Rice Round-Up

Slow Cooker Pepper Steak

2 tablespoons vegetable oil
3 pounds boneless beef top sirloin steak, cut into strips
1 tablespoon minced garlic (5 to 6 cloves)
1 medium onion, chopped
½ cup reduced-sodium soy sauce
2 teaspoons sugar
1 teaspoon salt
½ teaspoon ground ginger
½ teaspoon black pepper
3 green bell peppers, cut into strips
¼ cup cold water
1 tablespoon cornstarch
Hot cooked white rice

Slow Cooker Directions

1. Heat oil in large skillet over medium-low heat. Brown steak strips. Add garlic; cook and stir 2 minutes. Transfer steak strips, garlic and pan juices to slow cooker.

2. Add onion, soy sauce, sugar, salt, ginger and black pepper to slow cooker; mix well. Cover; cook on LOW 6 to 8 hours or until meat is tender (up to 10 hours).

3. Add bell pepper strips during final hour of cooking. Before serving, mix together water and cornstarch; stir mixture into juices in slow cooker. Cook on HIGH 10 minutes or until thickened. Serve with rice.   *Makes 6 to 8 servings*

Slow Cooker Pepper Steak

Tacos in Pasta Shells

1 package (3 ounces) cream cheese with chives
18 jumbo pasta shells
1¼ pounds ground beef
1 teaspoon salt
1 teaspoon chili powder
2 tablespoons butter, melted
1 cup prepared taco sauce
1 cup (4 ounces) shredded Cheddar cheese
1 cup (4 ounces) shredded Monterey Jack cheese
1½ cups crushed tortilla chips
1 cup sour cream
3 green onions, chopped
Leaf lettuce, small pitted ripe olives and cherry tomatoes for garnish

1. Cut cream cheese into ½-inch cubes. Let stand at room temperature until softened. Cook pasta according to package directions. Place in colander and rinse under warm running water. Drain well. Return to saucepan.

2. Preheat oven to 350°F. Butter 13×9-inch baking pan.

3. Cook beef in large skillet over medium-high heat until brown, stirring to separate meat; drain drippings. Reduce heat to medium-low. Add cream cheese, salt and chili powder; simmer 5 minutes.

4. Toss shells with butter. Fill shells with beef mixture. Arrange shells in prepared pan. Pour taco sauce over each shell. Cover with foil.

5. Bake 15 minutes. Uncover; top with Cheddar cheese, Monterey Jack cheese and chips. Bake 15 minutes more or until bubbly. Top with sour cream and onions. Garnish, if desired.

Makes 4 to 6 servings

Tacos in Pasta Shells

Smothered Steak

   4 to 6 beef cubed steaks (about 1½ to 2 pounds)
      All-purpose flour
   1 can (10¾ ounces) condensed cream of mushroom soup, undiluted
   1 package (1 ounce) dry onion soup mix
      Hot cooked rice (optional)

Slow Cooker Directions

1. Dust steak lightly with flour. Place in slow cooker.

2. Combine soup and soup mix in medium bowl. Pour over steak. Cover; cook on LOW 6 to 8 hours. Serve over rice, if desired.   *Makes 4 servings*

Beef & Bean Burritos

      Nonstick cooking spray
   ½ pound beef round steak, cut into ½-inch pieces
   3 cloves garlic, minced
   1 can (about 15 ounces) pinto beans, rinsed and drained
   1 can (4 ounces) diced mild green chilies, drained
   ¼ cup finely chopped fresh cilantro
   6 (6-inch) flour tortillas, warmed
   ½ cup (2 ounces) shredded Cheddar cheese
      Salsa and sour cream (optional)

1. Spray nonstick skillet with cooking spray; heat over medium heat until hot. Add steak and garlic; cook and stir 5 minutes or until steak is cooked to desired doneness.

2. Stir beans, chilies and cilantro into skillet; cook and stir 5 minutes or until heated through.

3. Spoon steak mixture evenly down center of each tortilla; sprinkle cheese evenly over each tortilla. Fold bottom end of tortilla over filling; roll to enclose. Serve with salsa and sour cream, if desired.   *Makes 6 servings*

Rainbow Casserole

5 potatoes, peeled and cut into thin slices
1 pound ground beef
1 onion, peeled, halved and cut into thin slices
Salt and pepper
1 can (about 28 ounces) stewed tomatoes, drained, juice reserved
1 cup frozen peas *or* 1 can (about 6 ounces) peas

1. Preheat oven to 350°F. Spray 3-quart casserole with nonstick cooking spray.

2. Boil potatoes in salted water in large saucepan until almost tender. Drain and reserve. Meanwhile, cook and stir ground beef in medium skillet until no longer pink. Drain fat.

3. Layer ½ of ground beef, ½ of potatoes, ½ of onion, salt and pepper, ½ of tomatoes and ½ of peas. Repeat layers. Add reserved tomato juice.

4. Bake, covered, about 40 minutes or until most of liquid is absorbed.

Makes 4 to 6 servings

Peppered Beef Tips

1 pound beef round tip or round steaks
2 cloves garlic, minced
Black pepper
1 can (10¾ ounces) condensed French onion soup, undiluted
1 can (10¾ ounces) condensed cream of mushroom soup, undiluted
Hot cooked noodles or rice

Slow Cooker Directions
Place steaks into slow cooker. Sprinkle with garlic and pepper. Pour soups over beef. Cover; cook on LOW 8 to 10 hours. Serve over noodles or rice.

Makes 2 to 3 servings

Braciola

    1 can (28 ounces) tomato sauce
2½ teaspoons dried oregano leaves, divided
1¼ teaspoons dried basil leaves, divided
    1 teaspoon salt
    ½ pound bulk hot Italian sausage
    ½ cup chopped onion
    ¼ cup grated Parmesan cheese
    2 cloves garlic, minced
    1 tablespoon dried parsley flakes
    1 to 2 beef flank steaks (about 2½ pounds)

Slow Cooker Directions

1. Combine tomato sauce, 2 teaspoons oregano, 1 teaspoon basil and salt in medium bowl; set aside.

2. Cook sausage in large nonstick skillet over medium-high heat until no longer pink, stirring to separate; drain well. Combine sausage, onion, cheese, garlic, parsley, remaining ½ teaspoon oregano and ¼ teaspoon basil in medium bowl; set aside.

3. Place steak on countertop between two pieces waxed paper. Pound with meat mallet until steak is ⅛ to ¼ inch thick. Cut steak into about 3-inch wide strips.

4. Spoon sausage mixture evenly onto each steak strip. Roll up, jelly-roll style, securing meat with toothpicks. Place each roll in slow cooker. Pour reserved tomato sauce mixture over meat. Cover; cook on LOW 6 to 8 hours.

5. Cut each roll into slices. Arrange slices on dinner plates. Top with hot tomato sauce.
Makes 8 servings

Prep Time: 35 minutes
Cook Time: 6 to 8 hours

Braciola

Szechwan Beef Lo Mein

1 boneless beef top sirloin steak (about 1 pound)
4 cloves garlic, minced
2 teaspoons minced fresh ginger
¾ teaspoon red pepper flakes, divided
1 tablespoon vegetable oil
1 can (about 14 ounces) vegetable broth
1 cup water
2 tablespoons reduced-sodium soy sauce
1 package (8 ounces) frozen mixed vegetables for stir-fry
1 package (9 ounces) refrigerated angel hair pasta
¼ cup chopped fresh cilantro (optional)

1. Cut steak lengthwise in half, then crosswise into thin slices. Toss steak with garlic, ginger and ½ teaspoon red pepper flakes.

2. Heat oil in large nonstick skillet over medium-high heat. Add half of beef to skillet; stir-fry 2 minutes or until meat is barely pink in center. Remove from skillet; set aside. Repeat with remaining beef.

3. Add vegetable broth, water, soy sauce and remaining ¼ teaspoon red pepper flakes to skillet; bring to a boil over high heat. Add vegetables; return to a boil. Reduce heat to low; simmer, covered, 3 minutes or until vegetables are crisp-tender.

4. Uncover; stir in pasta. Return to a boil over high heat. Reduce heat to medium; simmer, uncovered, 2 minutes, separating pasta with two forks. Return steak and any accumulated juices to skillet; simmer 1 minute or until pasta is tender and steak is hot. Sprinkle with cilantro, if desired. *Makes 4 servings*

Szechwan Beef Lo Mein

Yankee Pot Roast and Vegetables

    1 beef chuck pot roast (2½ pounds)
       Salt and black pepper
    3 medium baking potatoes (about 1 pound), unpeeled and cut into
       quarters
    2 large carrots, cut into ¾-inch slices
    2 ribs celery, cut into ¾-inch slices
    1 medium onion, sliced
    1 large parsnip, cut into ¾-inch slices
    2 bay leaves
    1 teaspoon dried rosemary
    ½ teaspoon dried thyme leaves
    ½ cup reduced-sodium beef broth

Slow Cooker Directions

1. Trim excess fat from meat and discard. Cut meat into serving-size pieces; sprinkle with salt and pepper.

2. Combine vegetables, bay leaves, rosemary and thyme in slow cooker. Place beef over vegetables. Pour broth over beef. Cover; cook on LOW 8½ to 9 hours or until beef is fork-tender.

3. Remove beef to serving platter. Arrange vegetables around beef. Remove and discard bay leaves.   *Makes 10 to 12 servings*

Cook's Nook: To make gravy, ladle the juices into a 2-cup measure; let stand 5 minutes. Skim off and discard fat. Measure remaining juices and heat to a boil in small saucepan. For each cup of juice, mix 2 tablespoons of flour with ¼ cup of cold water until smooth. Stir mixture into boiling juices, stirring constantly 1 minute or until thickened.

Prep Time: 10 minutes
Cook Time: 8½ hours

Yankee Pot Roast and Vegetables

Zesty Italian Stuffed Peppers

3 bell peppers (green, red or yellow)
1 pound ground beef
1 jar (14 ounces) spaghetti sauce
1⅓ cups *French's*® French Fried Onions, divided
2 tablespoons *Frank's*® *RedHot*® Original Cayenne Pepper Sauce
½ cup uncooked instant rice
¼ cup sliced ripe olives
1 cup (4 ounces) shredded mozzarella cheese

Preheat oven to 400°F. Cut bell peppers in half lengthwise through stems; discard seeds. Place pepper halves, cut side up, in shallow 2-quart baking dish; set aside.

Place beef in large microwavable bowl. Microwave on HIGH 5 minutes or until meat is browned, stirring once. Drain. Stir in spaghetti sauce, ⅔ cup French Fried Onions, **Frank's RedHot** Sauce, rice and olives. Spoon evenly into bell pepper halves.

Cover; bake 35 minutes or until bell peppers are tender. Uncover; sprinkle with cheese and remaining ⅔ cup onions. Bake 1 minute or until onions are golden.

Makes 6 servings

Prep Time: 10 minutes
Cook Time: 36 minutes

Zesty Italian Stuffed Pepper

Fiesta Beef Enchiladas

8 ounces 95% lean ground beef
½ cup sliced green onions
2 teaspoons minced garlic
1 cup cold cooked white or brown rice
1½ cups chopped tomato, divided
¾ cup frozen corn, thawed
1 cup (4 ounces) shredded reduced-fat Mexican cheese blend or
      Cheddar cheese, divided
½ cup salsa or picante sauce
12 (6- to 7-inch) corn tortillas
1 can (10 ounces) mild or hot enchilada sauce
1 cup shredded romaine lettuce

1. Preheat oven to 375°F. Spray 13×9-inch baking dish with nonstick cooking spray; set aside.

2. Cook ground beef in medium nonstick skillet over medium heat until no longer pink; drain. Add green onions and garlic; cook and stir 2 minutes.

3. Add rice, 1 cup tomato, corn, ½ cup cheese and salsa to meat mixture; mix well. Spoon mixture down center of tortillas; roll up. Place enchiladas seam side down in prepared dish. Spoon enchilada sauce evenly over top.

4. Cover with foil; bake 20 minutes or until hot. Sprinkle with remaining ½ cup cheese; bake 5 minutes or until cheese melts. Top with lettuce and remaining ½ cup tomato.   *Makes 6 servings*

Prep Time: 15 minutes
Cook Time: 35 minutes

Fiesta Beef Enchiladas

Beef and Parsnip Stroganoff

1 beef bouillon cube
¾ cup boiling water
1 boneless beef top round steak (about ¾ pound), trimmed
  Nonstick olive oil cooking spray
2 cups cubed peeled parsnips or potatoes*
1 medium onion, halved and thinly sliced
¾ pound mushrooms, sliced
2 teaspoons minced garlic
¼ teaspoon black pepper
¼ cup water
1 tablespoon plus 1½ teaspoons all-purpose flour
3 tablespoons reduced-fat sour cream
1½ teaspoons Dijon mustard
¼ teaspoon cornstarch
1 tablespoon chopped fresh parsley
4 ounces uncooked yolk-free wide noodles, cooked without salt,
  drained and kept hot

*If using potatoes, cut into 1-inch chunks and do not sauté.

Slow Cooker Directions

1. Dissolve bouillon cube in ¾ cup boiling water; cool. Meanwhile, cut steak lengthwise in half, then crosswise into ½-inch strips. Spray large nonstick skillet with cooking spray; heat over high heat. Add beef; cook and stir about 4 minutes or until meat begins to brown. Transfer beef and juices to slow cooker.

2. Spray same skillet with cooking spray; heat over high heat. Add parsnips and onion; cook and stir about 4 minutes or until browned. Add mushrooms, garlic and pepper; cook and stir about 5 minutes or until mushrooms are tender. Transfer mixture to slow cooker.

3. Stir ¼ cup water into flour in small bowl until smooth. Stir flour mixture into cooled bouillon. Add to slow cooker; stir until blended. Cover; cook on LOW 4½ to 5 hours or until beef and parsnips are tender.

4. Turn off slow cooker. Remove beef and vegetables with slotted spoon to large bowl; reserve cooking liquid from beef. Blend sour cream, mustard and cornstarch in medium bowl. Gradually add reserved liquid to sour cream mixture; stir well to blend. Stir sour cream mixture into beef and vegetable mixture. Sprinkle with parsley; serve over hot noodles. Garnish, if desired.   *Makes 4 servings*

Round Steak

**1 boneless beef round steak (1½ pounds), trimmed and cut into
   4 pieces**
¼ cup all-purpose flour
1 teaspoon black pepper
½ teaspoon salt
1 tablespoon vegetable oil
1 can (10¾ ounces) condensed cream of mushroom soup, undiluted
¾ cup water
1 medium onion, quartered
1 can (4 ounces) sliced mushrooms, drained
¼ cup milk
1 package (1 ounce) dry onion soup mix
1 bay leaf
   Salt
   Black pepper
   Ground sage
   Dried thyme leaves

Slow Cooker Directions

1. Place steaks in large resealable plastic food storage bag. Close bag and pound with meat mallet to tenderize. Combine flour, 1 teaspoon pepper and ½ teaspoon salt in small bowl; add to bag with steaks. Shake to coat meat evenly. Heat oil in large nonstick skillet. Remove steaks from bag; shake off excess flour. Add steaks to skillet; brown both sides.

2. Transfer steaks and pan juices to slow cooker. Add canned soup, water, onion, mushrooms, milk, dry soup mix, bay leaf and seasonings to taste to slow cooker; mix well.

3. Cover; cook on LOW 5 to 6 hours or until steak is tender. Remove and discard bay leaf before serving. *Makes 4 servings*

Beef Bourguignon

    1 to 2 boneless beef top sirloin steaks (about 3 pounds)
½ cup all-purpose flour
    4 slices bacon, diced
    2 medium carrots, diced
    8 small new red potatoes, unpeeled, cut into quarters
    8 to 10 mushrooms, sliced
20 to 24 pearl onions
    3 cloves garlic, minced
    1 bay leaf
    1 teaspoon dried marjoram leaves
½ teaspoon dried thyme leaves
½ teaspoon salt
    Black pepper
2½ cups Burgundy wine or beef broth

Slow Cooker Directions

1. Cut beef into ½-inch pieces. Coat with flour, shaking off excess; set aside. Cook bacon in large skillet over medium heat until partially cooked. Add beef; cook until browned. Remove beef and bacon with slotted spoon.

2. Layer carrots, potatoes, mushrooms, onions, garlic, bay leaf, marjoram, thyme, salt, pepper to taste and beef and bacon mixture in slow cooker. Pour wine over top.

3. Cover; cook on LOW 8 to 9 hours or until beef is tender. Remove and discard bay leaf before serving. *Makes 10 to 12 servings*

Beef Bourguignon

Mom's Spaghetti Sauce

7½ cups water
   3 cans (15 ounces each) tomato puree
   3 cans (6 ounces each) tomato paste*
   1 can (14½ ounces) tomatoes, undrained
   2 large onions, chopped
   3 tablespoons sugar
   2 tablespoons salt
1½ tablespoons Italian seasoning
1½ tablespoons dried oregano
   1 tablespoon black pepper
   6 large cloves garlic, minced
   3 bay leaves
   2 to 2½ pounds Italian hot or sweet sausage (optional)
   3 pounds ground beef, shaped into about 35 meatballs and browned (optional)

*Add more tomato paste if sauce is not thick enough for your taste.

Slow Cooker Directions

1. Combine all ingredients, except optional sausage and meatballs, in slow cooker; mix well. If using optional sausage and meatballs, divide sauce between two slow cookers.

2. Cover; cook on HIGH 1 hour. Add meatballs and sausages to each slow cooker, if desired. Cover; cook on LOW 6 to 8 hours. *Makes 10 to 12 servings*

Mom's Spaghetti Sauce

Manicotti

1 container (16 ounces) ricotta cheese
2 cups (8 ounces) shredded mozzarella cheese
½ cup cottage cheese
2 tablespoons grated Parmesan cheese
2 eggs, beaten
½ teaspoon minced garlic
   Salt and black pepper
1 package (about 8 ounces) uncooked manicotti shells
1 pound ground beef
1 jar (26 ounces) spaghetti sauce
2 cups water

1. Combine ricotta cheese, mozzarella cheese, cottage cheese, Parmesan cheese, eggs and garlic in large bowl; mix well. Season with salt and pepper.

2. Stuff mixture into uncooked manicotti shells, using narrow rubber spatula. Place filled shells in 13×9-inch baking dish. Preheat oven to 375°F.

3. Cook ground beef in large skillet over medium-high heat until no longer pink, stirring to separate. Drain excess fat. Stir in spaghetti sauce and water (mixture will be thin). Pour sauce over filled manicotti shells.

4. Cover with foil; bake 1 hour or until sauce has thickened and shells are tender.

Makes 6 servings

Manicotti

Easy Beef Stroganoff

3 cans (10¾ ounces each) condensed cream of chicken or cream of mushroom soup, undiluted
1 cup sour cream
½ cup water
1 package (1 ounce) dry onion soup mix
2 pounds beef for stew

Slow Cooker Directions

Combine soup, sour cream, water and dry soup mix in slow cooker. Add beef; stir until well coated. Cover; cook on on LOW 6 hours or HIGH 3 hours.

Makes 4 to 6 servings

Autumn Delight

4 to 6 beef cubed steaks
   Olive oil
2 to 3 cans (10¾ ounces each) condensed cream of mushroom soup, undiluted
1 to 1½ cups water
1 package (1 ounce) dry onion soup mix or mushroom soup mix

Slow Cooker Directions

1. Lightly brown cubed steaks in oil in large nonstick skillet over medium heat. Place steaks in slow cooker.

2. Add soup, water (½ cup water per can of soup) and soup mix to slow cooker; stir to combine. Cover; cook on LOW 4 to 6 hours. *Makes 4 to 6 servings*

Easy Beef Stroganoff

Biscuit-Topped Hearty Steak Pie

1½ **pounds top round steak, cooked and cut into 1-inch cubes**
1 **package (9 ounces) frozen baby carrots**
1 **package (9 ounces) frozen peas and pearl onions**
1 **large baking potato, cooked and cut into ½-inch pieces**
1 **jar (18 ounces) home-style brown gravy**
½ **teaspoon dried thyme leaves**
½ **teaspoon black pepper**
1 **can (10 ounces) flaky buttermilk biscuits**

Preheat oven to 375°F. Spray 2-quart casserole with nonstick cooking spray.

Combine steak, frozen vegetables and potato in prepared dish. Stir in gravy, thyme and pepper.

Bake, uncovered, 40 minutes. Remove from oven. *Increase oven temperature to 400°F.* Top with biscuits and bake 8 to 10 minutes or until biscuits are golden brown.
Makes 6 servings

Hint: This casserole can be prepared with leftovers of almost any kind. Other steaks, roast beef, stew meat, pork, lamb or chicken can be substituted for round steak; adjust gravy flavor to complement meat. Red potatoes can be used in place of baking potato. Choose your favorite vegetable combination, such as broccoli, cauliflower and carrots, or broccoli, corn and red peppers, as a substitute for the peas and carrots.

Biscuit-Topped Hearty Steak Pie

Classic Beef & Noodles

    2 pounds beef for stew, cut into 1-inch pieces
  1/4 pound mushrooms, sliced into halves
    2 tablespoons chopped onion
    2 cloves garlic, minced
    1 teaspoon salt
    1 teaspoon dried oregano leaves
  1/2 teaspoon black pepper
  1/4 teaspoon dried marjoram leaves
    1 bay leaf
1 1/2 cups beef broth
  1/3 cup dry sherry
    1 container (8 ounces) sour cream
  1/2 cup all-purpose flour
  1/4 cup water
    4 cups hot cooked noodles

Slow Cooker Directions

1. Heat oil in large skillet. Brown beef on all sides. (Work in batches, if necessary.) Drain and discard fat.

2. Combine beef, mushrooms, onion, garlic, salt, oregano, pepper, marjoram and bay leaf in slow cooker. Pour in beef broth and sherry. Cover; cook on LOW 8 to 10 hours or on HIGH 4 to 5 hours. Remove and discard bay leaf.

3. If cooking on LOW, turn to HIGH. Stir together sour cream, flour and water in small bowl. Stir about 1 cup liquid from slow cooker into sour cream mixture. Stir mixture back into slow cooker. Cover; cook on HIGH 30 minutes or until thickened and bubbly. Serve over noodles. Garnish as desired. *Makes 8 servings*

Classic Beef & Noodles

Deviled Beef Short Rib Stew

4 pounds beef short ribs, trimmed
2 pounds small red potatoes, scrubbed and scored
8 carrots, peeled and cut into chunks
2 onions, cut into thick wedges
1 bottle (12 ounces) beer or non-alcoholic malt beverage
8 tablespoons *French's*® Bold n' Spicy Brown Mustard, divided
3 tablespoons *French's*® Worcestershire Sauce, divided
2 tablespoons cornstarch

Slow Cooker Directions

1. Broil ribs 6 inches from heat on rack in broiler pan 10 minutes or until well browned, turning once. Place vegetables in bottom of slow cooker. Place ribs on top of vegetables.

2. Combine beer, *6 tablespoons* mustard and *2 tablespoons* Worcestershire in medium bowl. Pour into slow cooker. Cover and cook on high 5 hours* or until meat is tender.

3. Transfer meat and vegetables to platter; keep warm. Strain fat from broth; pour broth into saucepan. Combine cornstarch with *2 tablespoons cold water* in small bowl. Stir into broth with remaining *2 tablespoons* mustard and *1 tablespoon* Worcestershire. Heat to boiling. Reduce heat to medium-low. Cook 1 to 2 minutes or until thickened, stirring often. Pass gravy with meat and vegetables. Serve meat with additional mustard. *Makes 6 servings (with 3 cups gravy)*

Or cook 10 hours on low.

Tip: Prepare ingredients the night before for quick assembly in the morning. Keep refrigerated until ready to use.

Slow Cooker Meatloaf

1½ pounds ground beef
¾ cup milk
⅔ cup fine dry bread crumbs
2 eggs, beaten
2 tablespoons minced onion
1 teaspoon salt
½ teaspoon ground sage
½ cup ketchup
2 tablespoons brown sugar
1 teaspoon dry mustard

Slow Cooker Directions

1. Combine beef, milk, bread crumbs, eggs, onion, salt and sage in large bowl. Shape into ball and place in slow cooker. Cover; cook on LOW 5 to 6 hours.

2. Fifteen minutes before serving, combine ketchup, brown sugar and mustard in small bowl. Pour over meatloaf. Cover; cook on HIGH 15 minutes.

Makes 6 servings

Beef Roll-Ups

1 boneless beef round steak (1½ pounds), ½ inch thick
4 slices bacon
½ cup diced green bell pepper
¼ cup diced onion
¼ cup diced celery
1 can (10 ounces) beef gravy

Slow Cooker Directions

1. Cut steak into 4 pieces. Place 1 bacon slice on each piece.

2. Combine bell pepper, onion and celery in medium bowl. Place about ¼ cup mixture on each piece of meat. Roll up meat; secure with toothpicks.

3. Place beef rolls in slow cooker. Pour gravy evenly over top. Cover; cook on LOW 8 to 10 hours. Skim and discard fat before serving. *Makes 4 servings*

Slow Cooker Stuffed Peppers

1 package (about 7 ounces) Spanish rice mix
1 pound ground beef
½ cup diced celery
1 small onion, chopped
1 egg, beaten
4 medium green bell peppers, halved lengthwise, cored and seeded
1 can (28 ounces) whole peeled tomatoes, undrained
1 can (10¾ ounces) condensed tomato soup, undiluted
1 cup water

Slow Cooker Directions

1. Set aside seasoning packet from rice. Combine beef, rice mix, celery, onion and egg in large bowl. Divide meat mixture evenly among pepper halves.

2. Pour tomatoes with juice into slow cooker. Arrange filled pepper halves on top of tomatoes. Combine tomato soup, water and reserved rice mix seasoning packet in medium bowl. Pour over peppers. Cover; cook on LOW 8 to 10 hours.

Makes 4 servings

Corned Beef and Cabbage

1 head cabbage (1½ pounds), cut into 6 wedges
4 ounces baby carrots
1 corned beef (3 pounds) with seasoning packet*
1 quart (4 cups) water
⅓ cup prepared mustard (optional)
⅓ cup honey (optional)

*If seasoning packet is not perforated, poke several small holes with tip of paring knife.

Slow Cooker Directions

1. Place cabbage in slow cooker; top with carrots.

2. Place seasoning packet on top of vegetables. Place corned beef, fat side up, over seasoning packet and vegetables. Add water. Cover; cook on LOW 10 hours.

3. Discard seasoning packet. Just before serving, combine mustard and honey in small bowl. Use as dipping sauce, if desired. *Makes 6 servings*

Slow Cooker Stuffed Peppers

Beef Picante and Sour Cream Casserole

        6 ounces uncooked wagon wheel pasta
        8 ounces 95% lean ground beef
    1½ cups reduced-sodium mild picante sauce
        1 cup red kidney beans, rinsed and drained
        ¾ cup water
        1 tablespoon chili powder
        1 teaspoon ground cumin
        ½ cup fat-free cottage cheese
        ½ cup fat-free sour cream
        ½ cup chopped green onions, with tops
        1 can (2¼ ounces) sliced black olives
        ¼ cup chopped fresh cilantro or fresh parsley

1. Preheat oven to 325°F. Spray 9-inch square baking pan with nonstick cooking spray; set aside. Cook pasta according to package directions, omitting salt. Drain. Place in bottom of prepared pan; set aside.

2. Brown beef in large nonstick skillet over medium-high heat 4 to 5 minutes or until no longer pink, stirring to separate meat; drain fat.

3. Add picante sauce, beans, water, chili powder and cumin; blend well. Bring to a boil over high heat. Reduce heat to low; simmer, covered, 20 minutes.

4. Combine cottage cheese, sour cream and green onions in food processor or blender; process until smooth. Spread cottage cheese mixture over pasta in prepared pan. Spoon meat mixture over cottage cheese mixture; cover with foil. Bake 20 minutes or until heated through. Remove from oven; let stand 10 minutes to allow flavors to blend. Top with olives and cilantro.   *Makes 4 servings*

Steak San Marino

¼ **cup all-purpose flour**
1 **teaspoon salt**
½ **teaspoon black pepper**
1 **beef round steak (about 1½ pounds), cut into 4 pieces** *or* **2 beef top round steaks, cut in half**
1 **can (8 ounces) tomato sauce**
2 **carrots, chopped**
½ **onion, chopped**
1 **rib celery, chopped**
1 **teaspoon dried Italian seasoning**
½ **teaspoon Worcestershire sauce**
1 **bay leaf**
 Hot cooked rice

Slow Cooker Directions

1. Combine flour, salt and pepper in small bowl. Dredge each steak in flour mixture. Place in slow cooker. Combine tomato sauce, carrots, onion, celery, Italian seasoning, Worcestershire sauce and bay leaf in small bowl; pour into slow cooker.

2. Cover; cook on LOW 8 to 10 hours or on HIGH 4 to 5 hours.

3. Remove and discard bay leaf. Serve steaks and sauce over rice.

Makes 4 servings

Beef in Wine Sauce

4 pounds boneless beef chuck roast, cut into 1½- to 2-inch cubes
2 tablespoons garlic powder
2 cans (10¾ ounces each) condensed golden mushroom soup, undiluted
1 can (8 ounces) sliced mushrooms, drained
¾ cup dry sherry
1 envelope (about 1 ounce) dry onion soup mix
1 bag (20 ounces) frozen sliced carrots, thawed

1. Preheat oven to 325°F. Spray heavy 4-quart casserole or Dutch oven with nonstick cooking spray.

2. Sprinkle beef with garlic powder. Place in prepared casserole.

3. Combine canned soup, mushrooms, sherry and dry soup mix in medium bowl. Pour over meat; mix well.

4. Cover; bake 3 hours or until meat is very tender. Add carrots during last 15 minutes of baking. *Makes 6 to 8 servings*

Beef in Wine Sauce

Old-Fashioned Beef Pot Pie

1 pound ground beef
1 can (11 ounces) condensed beef with vegetables and barley soup
½ cup water
1 package (10 ounces) frozen peas and carrots, thawed and drained
½ teaspoon seasoned salt
⅛ teaspoon garlic powder
⅛ teaspoon ground black pepper
1 cup (4 ounces) shredded Cheddar cheese, divided
1⅓ cups *French's*® French Fried Onions, divided
1 package (7½ ounces) refrigerated biscuits

Preheat oven to 350°F. In large skillet, brown ground beef in large chunks; drain. Stir in soup, water, vegetables and seasonings; bring to a boil. Reduce heat and simmer, uncovered, 5 minutes. Remove from heat; stir in ½ cup cheese and ⅔ *cup* French Fried Onions.

Pour mixture into 12×8-inch baking dish. Cut each biscuit in half; place, cut side down, around edge of casserole. Bake, uncovered, 15 to 20 minutes or until biscuits are done. Top with remaining cheese and ⅔ *cup* onions; bake, uncovered, 5 minutes or until onions are golden brown.   *Makes 4 to 6 servings*

Old-Fashioned Beef Pot Pie

Quick Beef Bourguignonne

   3 tablespoons all-purpose flour
  ½ **teaspoon dried thyme**
  ½ **teaspoon ground black pepper**
  ¾ **pound boneless sirloin or top round steak, cut into 1-inch pieces**
   2 tablespoons vegetable oil, divided
   3 cups (8 ounces) halved or quartered crimini or white mushrooms
  ⅓ **cup thinly sliced shallots or chopped onion**
   1 (14½-ounce) can beef broth
  ¼ **cup water**
  ¼ **cup dry red wine or water**
   1 (4.8-ounce) package PASTA RONI® Garlic Alfredo
  ¾ **cup thinly sliced carrots**

1. Combine flour, thyme and pepper in resealable plastic food storage bag. Add steak; shake to coat evenly with flour mixture.

2. In large skillet over medium-high heat, heat 1 tablespoon oil. Add steak; cook 3 minutes or until lightly browned on all sides. Remove from skillet; set aside.

3. In same skillet over medium heat, heat remaining 1 tablespoon oil. Add mushrooms and shallots; cook 3 minutes, stirring occasionally.

4. Add beef broth, ¼ cup water and wine; bring to a boil. Add pasta, steak, carrots and Special Seasonings. Reduce heat to medium. Simmer 5 minutes or until pasta is tender. Let stand 5 minutes before serving. *Makes 4 servings*

Prep Time: 15 minutes
Cook Time: 20 minutes

Quick Beef Bourguignonne

Patchwork Casserole

2 pounds ground beef
2 cups chopped green bell pepper
1 cup chopped onion
2 pounds frozen Southern-style hash-brown potatoes, thawed
2 cans (8 ounces each) tomato sauce
1 cup water
1 can (6 ounces) tomato paste
1 teaspoon salt
½ teaspoon dried basil leaves
¼ teaspoon black pepper
1 pound pasteurized process American cheese, thinly sliced

1. Preheat oven to 350°F.

2. Brown beef in large skillet over medium heat about 10 minutes; drain off fat. Add bell pepper and onion; cook and stir until tender, about 4 minutes. Stir in potatoes, tomato sauce, water, tomato paste, salt, basil and black pepper.

3. Spoon half of mixture into 13×9×2-inch baking pan or 3-quart baking dish; top with half of cheese. Spoon remaining meat mixture evenly on top of cheese. Cover pan with aluminum foil. Bake 45 minutes.

4. Cut remaining cheese into decorative shapes; place on top of casserole. Let stand loosely covered until cheese melts, about 5 minutes.   *Makes 8 to 10 servings*

Patchwork Casserole

Bird is the Word

Greek-Style Chicken

  6 boneless skinless chicken thighs
½ teaspoon salt
½ teaspoon black pepper
  1 tablespoon olive oil
½ cup chicken broth
  1 lemon, thinly sliced
¼ cup pitted kalamata olives
½ teaspoon dried oregano leaves
  1 clove garlic, minced
    Hot cooked orzo or rice

Slow Cooker Directions

1. Remove visible fat from chicken; sprinkle chicken thighs with salt and pepper. Heat oil in large skillet over medium-high heat. Brown chicken on all sides. Place in slow cooker.

2. Add broth, lemon, olives, oregano and garlic to slow cooker.

3. Cover; cook on LOW 5 to 6 hours or until chicken is tender. Serve with orzo.

Makes 4 to 6 servings

Prep Time: 15 minutes
Cook Time: 5 to 6 hours

Greek-Style Chicken

Pineapple Chicken and Sweet Potatoes

⅔ cup plus 3 tablespoons all-purpose flour, divided
1 teaspoon salt
1 teaspoon ground nutmeg
½ teaspoon ground cinnamon
⅛ teaspoon onion powder
⅛ teaspoon black pepper
6 chicken breasts
3 sweet potatoes, peeled and sliced
1 can (10¾ ounces) condensed cream of chicken soup, undiluted
½ cup pineapple juice
¼ pound mushrooms, sliced
2 teaspoons packed light brown sugar
½ teaspoon grated orange peel
Hot cooked rice

Slow Cooker Directions

1. Combine ⅔ cup flour, salt, nutmeg, cinnamon, onion powder and black pepper in large bowl. Thoroughly coat chicken in flour mixture. Place sweet potatoes on bottom of slow cooker. Top with chicken.

2. Combine soup, pineapple juice, mushrooms, remaining 3 tablespoons flour, brown sugar and orange peel in medium bowl; stir well. Pour soup mixture into slow cooker.

3. Cover; cook on LOW 8 to 10 hours or on HIGH 3 to 4 hours. Serve chicken and sauce over rice. *Make 6 servings*

Pineapple Chicken and Sweet Potatoes

Green Chile Chicken Enchiladas

2 cups shredded cooked chicken
1½ cups (6 ounces) shredded Mexican cheese blend or Cheddar cheese, divided
½ cup HIDDEN VALLEY® The Original Ranch® Dressing
¼ cup sour cream
2 tablespoons canned diced green chiles, rinsed and drained
4 (9-to 10-inch) flour tortillas, warmed

Mix together chicken, ¾ cup cheese, dressing, sour cream and green chiles in medium bowl. Divide evenly down center of each tortilla. Roll up tortillas and place, seam side down, in 9-inch baking dish. Top with remaining ¾ cup cheese. Bake at 350°F. for 20 minutes or until cheese is melted and lightly browned.

Makes 4 servings

Note: Purchase rotisserie chicken at your favorite store to add great taste and save preparation time.

Green Chile Chicken Enchilada

Spinach Quiche

> **1 medium leek**
> **¼ cup butter or margarine**
> **2 cups finely chopped cooked chicken**
> **½ package (10 ounces) frozen chopped spinach or broccoli, cooked and drained**
> **1 unbaked ready-to-use pie crust (10 inches in diameter)**
> **1½ cups (6 ounces) shredded Swiss cheese**
> **1 tablespoon all-purpose flour**
> **4 eggs**
> **1½ cups half-and-half or evaporated milk**
> **2 tablespoons brandy**
> **½ teaspoon salt**
> **¼ teaspoon black pepper**
> **¼ teaspoon ground nutmeg**

1. Preheat oven to 375°F. Cut leek in half lengthwise; wash and trim, leaving 2 to 3 inches of green tops intact. Cut leek halves crosswise into thin slices. Place in small saucepan; add enough water to cover. Bring to a boil over high heat; reduce heat and simmer 5 minutes. Drain; reserve leek.

2. Melt butter in large skillet over medium heat. Add chicken; cook 5 minutes or until chicken is golden. Add spinach and leek to chicken mixture; cook 1 to 2 minutes longer. Remove from heat. Spoon chicken mixture into unbaked pie crust. Sprinkle cheese and flour over chicken mixture.

3. Combine eggs, half-and-half, brandy, salt, pepper and nutmeg in medium bowl. Pour egg mixture over cheese.

4. Bake 35 to 40 minutes or until knife inserted into center comes out clean. Let stand 5 minutes before serving. Serve hot or cold.   *Makes 6 servings*

Spinach Quiche

Saffron Chicken Risotto

1½ pounds boneless, skinless chicken breast
¼ teaspoon salt
⅛ teaspoon white pepper
1 tablespoon olive oil
1 cup sliced fresh mushrooms
½ cup sliced green onions
½ cup chopped red bell pepper
½ cup chopped celery
1 tablespoon butter
1 cup uncooked rice
   Pinch of ground saffron
⅓ cup dry white wine
2 cups chicken broth
3 cups water
⅓ cup grated Parmesan cheese
⅓ cup sliced black olives
⅓ cup heavy cream

Cut chicken into 1-inch chunks; season with salt and white pepper. Heat oil in large skillet over medium-high heat until hot. Add chicken, mushrooms, onions, red pepper and celery. Cook and stir until chicken is no longer pink in center. Remove chicken and vegetables; set aside. Melt butter in skillet until hot. Add rice and saffron; cook 2 to 3 minutes, stirring constantly. Add wine; stir until absorbed. Stir in 1 cup broth; cook, uncovered, until broth is absorbed, stirring frequently. Continue stirring and adding remaining 1 cup broth and water, one cup at a time; allow each cup to be absorbed before adding another, until rice is tender and has creamy consistency, about 25 to 30 minutes. Stir in cheese, olives, cream and chicken mixture; heat thoroughly. Serve immediately. *Makes 4 servings*

Tip: Medium grain rice will yield the best consistency for risottos, but long grain rice may be used.

Favorite recipe from **USA Rice**

Saffron Chicken Risotto

Heidi's Chicken Supreme

1 can (10¾ ounces) condensed cream of chicken soup, undiluted
1 package (1 ounce) dry onion soup mix
6 boneless skinless chicken breasts (about 1½ pounds)
½ cup imitation bacon bits *or* ½ pound bacon, crisp-cooked and crumbled
1 container (16 ounces) reduced-fat sour cream

Slow Cooker Directions

1. Spray slow cooker with nonstick cooking spray. Combine canned soup and dry soup mix in medium bowl; mix well. Layer chicken breasts and soup mixture in slow cooker. Sprinkle with bacon bits.

2. Cover; cook on LOW 8 hours or on HIGH 4 hours.

3. During last hour of cooking, stir in sour cream. *Makes 6 servings*

Broccoli, Chicken and Rice Casserole

1 box UNCLE BEN'S CHEF'S RECIPE® Broccoli Rice Au Gratin Supreme
2 cups boiling water
4 boneless, skinless chicken breasts (about 1 pound)
¼ teaspoon garlic powder
2 cups frozen broccoli
1 cup (4 ounces) reduced-fat shredded Cheddar cheese

1. Heat oven to 425°F. In 13×9-inch baking pan, combine rice and contents of seasoning packet. Add boiling water; mix well. Add chicken; sprinkle with garlic powder. Cover and bake 30 minutes.

2. Add broccoli and cheese; continue to bake, covered, 8 to 10 minutes or until chicken is no longer pink in center. *Makes 4 servings*

Chicken Enchilada Roll-Ups

1½ **pounds boneless skinless chicken breasts**
½ **cup plus 2 tablespoons all-purpose flour, divided**
½ **teaspoon salt**
 2 **tablespoons butter**
 1 **cup chicken broth**
 1 **small onion, diced**
¼ **to** ½ **cup canned jalapeño peppers, sliced**
½ **teaspoon dried oregano leaves**
 2 **tablespoons heavy cream or milk**
 6 **flour tortillas (7 to 8 inches)**
 6 **thin slices American cheese or American cheese with jalapeño**
   peppers

Slow Cooker Directions

1. Cut each chicken breast lengthwise into 2 or 3 strips. Combine ½ cup flour and salt in plastic food storage bag. Add chicken strips and shake to coat with flour mixture. Melt butter in large skillet over medium heat. Brown chicken strips in batches 2 to 3 minutes per side. Place chicken into slow cooker.

2. Add chicken broth to skillet and scrape up any browned bits. Pour broth mixture into slow cooker. Add onion, jalapeño peppers and oregano. Cover; cook on LOW 7 to 8 hours.

3. Combine remaining 2 tablespoons flour and cream in small bowl; stir to form paste. Stir into chicken mixture; cook on HIGH until thickened. Spoon chicken mixture onto center of flour tortillas. Top with 1 cheese slice. Fold up tortillas and serve.

Makes 6 servings

Tip: This rich creamy chicken mixture can also be served over cooked rice.

Prep Time: 20 minutes
Cook Time: 7 to 8 hours (LOW)

Escalloped Chicken

10 slices white bread, cubed
1½ cups cracker or dry bread crumbs, divided
4 cups cubed cooked chicken
3 cups chicken broth
1 cup chopped onion
1 cup chopped celery
1 can (8 ounces) sliced mushrooms, drained
1 jar (about 4 ounces) pimientos, diced
3 eggs, lightly beaten
Salt and black pepper
1 tablespoon margarine

1. Preheat oven to 350°F.

2. Combine bread cubes and 1 cup cracker crumbs in large mixing bowl. Add chicken, broth, onion, celery, mushrooms, pimientos and eggs; mix well. Season with salt and pepper; spoon into 2½-quart casserole.

3. Melt margarine in small saucepan. Add remaining ½ cup cracker crumbs and brown, stirring occasionally. Sprinkle crumbs over casserole.

4. Bake 1 hour or until hot and bubbly.   *Makes 6 servings*

Escalloped Chicken

Mile-High Enchilada Pie

8 (6-inch) corn tortillas
1 jar (12 ounces) prepared salsa
1 can (15½ ounces) kidney beans, rinsed and drained
1 cup shredded cooked chicken
1 cup shredded Monterey Jack cheese with jalapeño peppers

Slow Cooker Directions

Prepare foil handles for slow cooker (see below); place in slow cooker. Place 1 tortilla on bottom of slow cooker. Top with small amount of salsa, beans, chicken and cheese. Continue layering using remaining ingredients, ending with cheese. Cover; cook on LOW 6 to 8 hours or on HIGH 3 to 4 hours. Pull out by foil handles. Garnish with fresh cilantro and slice of red pepper, if desired. *Makes 4 to 6 servings*

Foil Handles: Tear off three 18×2-inch strips of heavy foil or use regular foil folded to double thickness. Crisscross foil strips in spoke design and place in slow cooker to make lifting of tortilla stack easier.

Mile-High Enchilada Pie

Italian-Style Chicken and Rice

1 tablespoon vegetable oil
4 boneless, skinless chicken breasts (about 1 pound)
2 cups low-fat reduced-sodium chicken broth
1 box (about 6 ounces) chicken-flavored rice mix
½ cup chopped red bell pepper
½ cup frozen peas, thawed
¼ cup Romano cheese

Heat oil in large skillet. Add chicken; cook over medium-high heat 10 to 15 minutes or until lightly browned on both sides.

Add broth, rice mix, bell pepper and peas; mix well. Bring to a boil. Cover; reduce heat and simmer 10 minutes or until chicken is no longer pink in center. Remove from heat. Sprinkle with cheese; let stand covered 5 minutes or until liquid is absorbed.

Makes 4 servings

Italian-Style Chicken and Rice

Hot & Sour Chicken

4 to 6 boneless skinless chicken breasts (about 1 to 1½ pounds)
1 package (1 ounce) dry hot-and-sour soup mix
1 cup chicken or vegetable broth

Slow Cooker Directions

Place chicken in slow cooker. Add soup mix and broth. Cover; cook on LOW 5 to 6 hours. Garnish as desired.   *Makes 4 to 6 servings*

Chicken Pot Pie with Onion Biscuits

1 package (1.8 ounces) classic white sauce mix
2¾ cups milk, divided
¼ teaspoon dried thyme leaves
1 package (10 ounces) frozen peas and carrots, thawed
1 package (10 ounces) roasted carved chicken breast, cut into bite-size pieces
1 cup all-purpose baking mix
1⅓ cups *French's*® French Fried Onions, divided
½ cup (2 ounces) shredded Cheddar cheese

1. Preheat oven to 400°F. Prepare white sauce mix according to package directions with 2¼ cups milk; stir in thyme. Mix vegetables, chicken and prepared white sauce in shallow 2-quart casserole.

2. Combine baking mix, ⅔ *cup* French Fried Onions and remaining ½ cup milk in medium bowl until blended. Drop 6 to 8 spoonfuls of dough over chicken mixture.

3. Bake 25 minutes or until biscuits are golden. Sprinkle biscuits with cheese and remaining onions. Bake 3 minutes or until cheese is melted and onions are golden.
Makes 6 servings

Tip: You may substitute 2 cups cut-up cooked chicken for the roasted, carved chicken breast.

Variation: For added Cheddar flavor, substitute ***French's*® Cheddar French Fried Onions** for the original flavor.

Hot & Sour Chicken

Creamy Chicken and Mushrooms

 1 teaspoon salt
½ teaspoon black pepper
¼ teaspoon paprika
 3 boneless skinless chicken breasts, cut up into large pieces
1½ cups sliced fresh mushrooms
½ cup sliced green onions
1¾ teaspoons chicken bouillon granules
 1 cup dry white wine
½ cup water
 1 can (5 ounces) evaporated milk
 5 teaspoons cornstarch
    Hot cooked rice

Slow Cooker Directions

1. Combine salt, pepper and paprika in small bowl; sprinkle over chicken.

2. Layer chicken, mushrooms, green onions and bouillon in slow cooker. Pour wine and water over top. Cover; cook on LOW 5 to 6 hours or on HIGH 3 hours. Remove chicken and vegetables to platter; cover to keep warm.

3. Combine evaporated milk and cornstarch in small saucepan, stirring until smooth. Add 2 cups liquid from slow cooker; bring to a boil. Boil 1 minute or until thickened, stirring constantly. Serve chicken over rice and top with sauce.

Makes 3 to 4 servings

Creamy Chicken and Mushrooms

Slow-Simmered Curried Chicken

1½ **cups chopped onions**
  1 **medium green bell pepper, chopped**
  1 **pound boneless skinless chicken breast or thighs, cut into bite-size**
      pieces
  1 **cup medium salsa**
  2 **teaspoons grated fresh ginger**
½ **teaspoon garlic powder**
½ **teaspoon red pepper flakes**
¼ **cup chopped fresh cilantro**
  1 **teaspoon sugar**
  1 **teaspoon curry powder**
¾ **teaspoon salt**
    Hot cooked rice

Slow Cooker Directions

1. Place onions and bell pepper in bottom of slow cooker. Top with chicken. Combine salsa, ginger, garlic powder and pepper flakes in small bowl; spoon over chicken.

2. Cover; cook on LOW 5 to 6 hours or until chicken is tender.

3. Combine cilantro, sugar, curry powder and salt in small bowl. Stir mixture into slow cooker. Cover; cook on HIGH 15 minutes or until hot. Serve with rice.

Makes 4 servings

Prep Time: 15 to 20 minutes
Cook Time: 5 to 6 hours (LOW)

Chicken Pot Pie

1 ½ **pounds chicken pieces, skinned**
 1 **cup chicken broth**
 ½ **teaspoon salt**
 ¼ **teaspoon black pepper**
 1 **to 1 ½ cups reduced-fat (2%) milk**
 3 **tablespoons butter**
 1 **medium onion, chopped**
 1 **cup sliced celery**
 ⅓ **cup all-purpose flour**
 2 **cups frozen mixed vegetables (broccoli, carrots and cauliflower combination), thawed**
 1 **tablespoon chopped fresh parsley** *or* 1 **teaspoon dried parsley**
 ½ **teaspoon dried thyme leaves**
 1 **(9-inch) refrigerated pastry crust**
 1 **egg, lightly beaten**

1. Combine chicken, chicken broth, salt and pepper in large saucepan over medium-high heat. Bring to a boil. Reduce heat to low. Cover; simmer 30 minutes or until juices run clear.

2. Remove chicken and let cool. Pour remaining chicken broth mixture into glass measure. Let stand; spoon off fat. Add enough milk to broth mixture to equal 2½ cups. Remove chicken from bones and cut into ½-inch pieces.

3. Melt butter in same saucepan over medium heat. Add onion and celery. Cook and stir 3 minutes. Stir in flour until well blended. Gradually stir in broth mixture. Cook, stirring constantly, until sauce thickens and boils. Add chicken, vegetables, parsley and thyme. Pour into 1½-quart deep casserole.

4. Preheat oven to 400°F. Roll out pastry 1 inch larger than diameter of casserole on lightly floured surface. Cut slits in pastry to vent; place on top of casserole. Roll edges and cut away extra pastry; flute edges. Reroll scraps to cut into decorative designs. Place on top of pastry. Brush pastry with beaten egg. Bake about 30 minutes until crust is golden brown and filling is bubbly. *Makes about 6 cups or 4 servings*

Cook's Nook: Two cups diced cooked chicken, 1 can (14½ ounces) chicken broth, ¼ teaspoon salt and ¼ teaspoon black pepper can be substituted for the first 4 ingredients.

Slow Cooker Chicken & Rice

3 cans (10¾ ounces each) condensed cream of chicken soup,
    undiluted
2 cups uncooked instant rice
1 cup water
1 pound boneless skinless chicken breasts or chicken breast tenders
½ teaspoon salt
¼ teaspoon black pepper
¼ teaspoon paprika
½ cup diced celery

Slow Cooker Directions

Combine soup, rice and water in slow cooker. Add chicken; sprinkle with salt, pepper
and paprika. Sprinkle celery over chicken. Cover; cook on LOW 6 to 8 hours or on
HIGH 3 to 4 hours.   *Makes 4 servings*

Slow Cooker Chicken & Rice

Swiss Melt Chicken

1 tablespoon olive oil
¼ cup minced onion
1 clove garlic, minced
4 boneless skinless chicken breasts
1 package (about 6 ounces) long grain and wild rice
1⅔ cups chicken broth
1 cup sliced mushrooms
½ cup chopped green bell pepper
½ cup chopped red bell pepper
4 slices Swiss cheese

1. Heat oil in large skillet over medium heat. Add onion and garlic; cook and stir 2 minutes or until onions are soft. Add chicken; cook 5 to 7 minutes until light brown, turning once. Add rice, contents of seasoning packet and broth. Bring to a boil. Cover; simmer 20 minutes or until rice is done.

2. Stir in mushrooms and bell peppers. Cook, covered, 5 to 8 minutes or until chicken is no longer pink in center and juices run clear when cut.

3. Place cheese over chicken; remove from heat. Let stand, covered, 5 minutes or until cheese is melted. Season to taste.   *Makes 4 servings*

Swiss Melt Chicken

San Marino Chicken

1 chicken (3 pounds), skinned and cut up
¼ cup all-purpose flour
1 can (8 ounces) tomato sauce
⅓ cup chopped sun-dried tomatoes packed in oil
¼ cup red wine
1 tablespoon grated lemon peel
2 cups sliced mushrooms
2 cups *French's*® French Fried Onions, divided
    Hot cooked rice or pasta (optional)

Slow Cooker Directions

1. Lightly coat chicken pieces with flour. Place chicken in slow cooker. Add tomato sauce, sun-dried tomatoes, wine and lemon peel. Cover and cook on LOW setting for 4 hours (or on HIGH for 2 hours).

2. Add mushrooms and *1 cup* French Fried Onions. Cover and cook on LOW setting for 2 hours (or on HIGH for 1 hour) until chicken is no longer pink near bone. Remove chicken to heated platter. Skim fat from sauce.

3. Serve chicken with hot cooked rice or pasta, if desired. Spoon sauce on top and sprinkle with remaining onions.   *Makes 4 servings*

Prep Time: 5 minutes
Cook Time: 6 hours

San Marino Chicken

3-Cheese Chicken & Noodles

3 cups chopped cooked chicken
1½ cups cottage cheese
1 can (10¾ ounces) condensed cream of chicken soup, undiluted
1 package (8 ounces) wide egg noodles, cooked and drained
1 cup grated Monterey Jack cheese
½ cup diced celery
½ cup diced onion
½ cup diced green bell pepper
½ cup diced red bell pepper
½ cup grated Parmesan cheese
½ cup chicken broth
1 can (4 ounces) sliced mushrooms, drained
2 tablespoons butter, melted
½ teaspoon dried thyme leaves

Slow Cooker Directions

Combine all ingredients in slow cooker. Stir to coat evenly. Cover; cook on LOW 6 to 10 hours or on HIGH 3 to 4 hours.   *Makes 6 servings*

3-Cheese Chicken & Noodles

Orange Ginger Chicken & Rice

1 package (6.9 ounces) RICE-A-RONI® With ⅓ Less Salt Chicken Flavor
1 tablespoon margarine or butter
1 cup orange juice
¾ pound skinless boneless chicken breasts, cut into thin strips
2 cloves garlic, minced
¼ teaspoon ground ginger
Dash red pepper flakes (optional)
1½ cups carrots, cut into short thin strips *or* 3 cups broccoli flowerets

1. In large skillet, sauté Rice-A-Roni® mix and margarine over medium heat, stirring frequently until vermicelli is golden brown.

2. Stir in 1½ cups water, orange juice, chicken, garlic, ginger, red pepper flakes and Special Seasonings; bring to a boil over high heat.

3. Cover; reduce heat. Simmer 10 minutes.

4. Stir in carrots.

5. Cover; continue to simmer 5 to 10 minutes or until liquid is absorbed and rice is tender.   *Makes 4 servings*

Orange Ginger Chicken & Rice

Oriental Chicken & Rice

1 (6.9-ounce) package RICE-A-RONI® Chicken Flavor
2 tablespoons margarine or butter
1 pound boneless, skinless chicken breasts, cut into thin strips
¼ cup teriyaki sauce
½ teaspoon ground ginger
1 (16-ounce) package frozen Oriental-style mixed vegetables

1. In large skillet over medium heat, sauté rice-vermicelli mix with margarine until vermicelli is golden brown.

2. Slowly stir in 2 cups water, chicken, teriyaki sauce, ginger and Special Seasonings; bring to a boil. Reduce heat to low. Cover; simmer 10 minutes.

3. Stir in vegetables. Cover; simmer 5 to 10 minutes or until rice is tender and chicken is no longer pink inside. Let stand 3 minutes.   *Makes 4 servings*

Prep Time: 5 minutes
Cook Time: 25 minutes

Oriental Chicken & Rice

Simple Coq au Vin

4 chicken legs
  Salt and black pepper
2 tablespoons olive oil
½ pound mushrooms, sliced
  1 onion, sliced into rings
½ cup red wine
½ teaspoon dried basil leaves
½ teaspoon dried thyme leaves
½ teaspoon dried oregano leaves
  Hot cooked rice

Slow Cooker Directions

1. Sprinkle chicken with salt and pepper. Heat oil in large skillet; brown chicken on both sides. Remove chicken and place in slow cooker. Sauté mushrooms and onion in same skillet. Add wine; stir and scrape brown bits from bottom of skillet. Add mixture to slow cooker. Sprinkle with basil, thyme and oregano.

2. Cover; cook on LOW 8 to 10 hours or on HIGH 3 to 4 hours.

3. Serve chicken and sauce over rice.   *Makes 4 servings*

Simple Coq au Vin

Curried Chicken, Vegetables and Couscous Skillet

1 package (16 ounces) frozen vegetable medley, such as broccoli, carrots and cauliflower or bell pepper and onion strips
1 pound chicken tenders
2 teaspoons curry powder, divided
¾ teaspoon garlic salt
⅛ teaspoon ground red pepper
4½ teaspoons vegetable oil
1 can (about 14 ounces) chicken broth
1 cup uncooked couscous

1. Thaw vegetables according to package directions.

2. While vegetables are thawing, place chicken in medium bowl. Sprinkle with 1 teaspoon curry powder, garlic salt and ground red pepper; toss to coat.

3. Heat oil in large deep skillet over medium-high heat until hot. Add chicken mixture, spreading in one layer. Cook 5 to 6 minutes or until chicken is no longer pink in center, turning occasionally.

4. Transfer chicken to plate; set aside. Add broth and remaining 1 teaspoon curry powder to skillet; bring to a boil over high heat, scraping up browned bits on bottom of skillet.

5. Stir thawed vegetables into skillet; return to a boil. Stir in couscous; top with chicken. Cover and remove from heat. Let stand 5 minutes or until liquid is absorbed.

Makes 4 servings

Note: For a special touch, add a dollop of plain yogurt to each serving.

Prep and Cook Time: 19 minutes

Tomato, Basil & Broccoli Chicken

4 boneless, skinless chicken breast halves
Salt and black pepper (optional)
2 tablespoons margarine or butter
1 package (6.9 ounces) RICE-A-RONI® Chicken Flavor
1 teaspoon dried basil leaves
2 cups broccoli florets
1 medium tomato, seeded, chopped
1 cup (4 ounces) shredded mozzarella cheese

1. Sprinkle chicken with salt and pepper, if desired.

2. In large skillet, melt margarine over medium-high heat. Add chicken; cook 2 minutes on each side or until browned. Remove from skillet; set aside, reserving drippings. Keep warm.

3. In same skillet, sauté rice-vermicelli mix in reserved drippings over medium heat until vermicelli is golden brown. Stir in 2½ cups water, Special Seasonings and basil. Place chicken over rice mixture; bring to a boil over high heat.

4. Cover; reduce heat. Simmer 15 minutes. Top with broccoli and tomato.

5. Cover; continue to simmer 5 minutes or until liquid is absorbed and chicken is no longer pink in center. Sprinkle with cheese. Cover; let stand a few minutes before serving.   *Makes 4 servings*

Artichoke-Olive Chicken Bake

1½ cups uncooked rotini
1 tablespoon olive oil
1 medium onion, chopped
½ green bell pepper, chopped
2 cups shredded cooked chicken
1 can (14½ ounces) diced tomatoes with Italian-style herbs, undrained
1 can (14 ounces) artichoke hearts, drained and quartered
1 can (6 ounces) sliced black olives, drained
1 teaspoon Italian seasoning
2 cups (8 ounces) shredded mozzarella cheese

Preheat oven to 350°F. Spray 2-quart casserole with nonstick cooking spray.

Cook pasta according to package directions until al dente. Drain and set aside.

Meanwhile, heat oil in large deep skillet over medium heat until hot. Add onion and pepper; cook and stir 1 minute. Add chicken, tomatoes with juice, pasta, artichokes, olives and Italian seasoning; mix until combined.

Place half of chicken mixture in prepared dish; sprinkle with half of cheese. Top with remaining chicken mixture and cheese.

Bake, covered, 35 minutes or until hot and bubbly.   *Makes 8 servings*

Artichoke-Olive Chicken Bake

Paella

¼ cup **FILIPPO BERIO**® **Olive Oil**
1 **pound boneless skinless chicken breasts, cut into 1-inch strips**
½ **pound Italian sausage, cut into 1-inch slices**
1 **onion, chopped**
3 **cloves garlic, minced**
2 **(14½-ounce) cans chicken broth**
2 **cups uncooked long grain white rice**
1 **(8-ounce) bottle clam juice**
1 **(2-ounce) jar chopped pimientos, drained**
2 **bay leaves**
1 **teaspoon salt**
¼ **teaspoon saffron threads, crumbled (optional)**
1 **pound raw shrimp, shelled and deveined**
1 **(16-ounce) can whole tomatoes, drained**
1 **(10-ounce) package frozen peas, thawed**
12 **littleneck clams, scrubbed**
¼ **cup water**
Fresh herb sprig (optional)

Preheat oven to 350°F. In large skillet, heat olive oil over medium heat until hot. Add chicken; cook and stir 8 to 10 minutes or until brown on all sides. Remove with slotted spoon; set aside. Add sausage to skillet; cook and stir 8 to 10 minutes or until brown. Remove with slotted spoon; set aside. Add onion and garlic to skillet; cook and stir 5 to 7 minutes or until onion is tender. Transfer chicken, sausage, onion and garlic mixture to large casserole.

Add chicken broth, rice, clam juice, pimientos, bay leaves, salt and saffron, if desired, to chicken mixture. Cover; bake 30 minutes. Add shrimp, tomatoes and peas; stir well. Cover; bake an additional 15 minutes or until rice is tender, liquid is absorbed and shrimp are opaque. Remove bay leaves.

Meanwhile, combine clams and water in stockpot or large saucepan. Cover; cook over medium heat 5 to 10 minutes or until clams open; remove clams immediately as they open. Discard any clams with unopened shells. Place clams on top of paella. Garnish with herb sprig, if desired. *Makes 4 to 6 servings*

Paella

Forty-Clove Chicken

  1 frying chicken (3 pounds), cut into serving pieces
    Salt and black pepper
  1 to 2 tablespoons olive oil
  ¼ cup dry white wine
  ⅛ cup dry vermouth
  2 tablespoons chopped fresh parsley *or* 2 teaspoons dried parsley
    flakes
  2 teaspoons dried basil leaves
  1 teaspoon dried oregano leaves
    Pinch of red pepper flakes
 40 cloves garlic (about 2 heads*), peeled
  4 ribs celery, sliced
    Juice and peel of 1 lemon
    Fresh herbs (optional)

The whole garlic bulb is called a head.

Slow Cooker Directions

1. Remove skin from chicken, if desired. Sprinkle chicken with salt and pepper. Heat oil in large skillet over medium heat. Add chicken; cook 10 minutes or until browned on all sides. Remove chicken from heat.

2. Combine wine, vermouth, parsley, basil, oregano and red pepper flakes in large bowl. Add garlic and celery; coat well. Transfer garlic and celery to slow cooker with slotted spoon. Add chicken to remaining herb mixture; coat well. Place chicken on top of celery in slow cooker. Sprinkle lemon juice and peel in slow cooker; add remaining herb mixture.

3. Cover and cook on LOW 6 hours or until chicken is no longer pink in center. Garnish with fresh herbs, if desired.   *Makes 4 to 6 servings*

Forty-Clove Chicken

Mexicali Chicken

2 medium green bell peppers, cut into thin strips
1 large onion, quartered and thinly sliced
4 chicken thighs
4 chicken drumsticks
1 tablespoon chili powder
2 teaspoons dried oregano leaves
1 jar (16 ounces) chipotle salsa
½ cup ketchup
2 teaspoons ground cumin
½ teaspoon salt
Hot cooked noodles

Slow Cooker Directions

1. Place bell peppers and onion in slow cooker; top with chicken. Sprinkle chili powder and oregano over chicken. Add salsa. Cover; cook on LOW 7 to 8 hours or until chicken is tender.

2. Remove chicken pieces to serving bowl; keep warm. Stir ketchup, cumin and salt into liquid in slow cooker. Cook, uncovered, on HIGH 15 minutes or until hot.

3. Pour mixture over chicken. Serve with noodles. *Makes 4 servings*

Tip: For thicker sauce, blend 1 tablespoon cornstarch and 2 tablespoons water. Stir into cooking liquid with ketchup, cumin and salt.

Prep Time: 10 minutes
Cook Time: 7 to 8 hours (LOW)

Mexicali Chicken

Coq au Vin & Pasta

**4 large or 8 small chicken thighs (2 to 2½ pounds), trimmed of
    excess fat
2 teaspoons rotisserie or herb chicken seasoning*
1 tablespoon margarine or butter
3 cups (8 ounces) halved or quartered mushrooms
1 medium onion, coarsely chopped
½ cup dry white wine or vermouth
1 (4.9-ounce) package PASTA RONI® Homestyle Chicken Flavor
½ cup sliced green onions**

*1 teaspoon paprika and 1 teaspoon garlic salt can be substituted.

1. Sprinkle meaty side of chicken with rotisserie seasoning. In large skillet
over medium-high heat, melt margarine. Add chicken, seasoned-side down;
cook 3 minutes. Reduce heat to medium-low; turn chicken over.

2. Add mushrooms, onion and wine. Cover; simmer 15 to 18 minutes or until
chicken is no longer pink inside. Remove chicken from skillet; set aside.

3. In same skillet, bring 1 cup water to a boil. Stir in pasta, green onions and
Special Seasonings. Place chicken over pasta. Reduce heat to medium-low. Cover;
gently boil 6 to 8 minutes or until pasta is tender. Let stand 3 to 5 minutes before
serving. *Makes 4 servings*

Prep Time: 10 minutes
Cook Time: 30 minutes

Coq au Vin & Pasta

Easy Chicken Alfredo

1½ **pounds chicken breast, cut into ½-inch pieces**
1 **medium onion, chopped**
1 **tablespoon dried chives**
1 **tablespoon dried basil leaves**
1 **tablespoon extra-virgin olive oil**
1 **teaspoon lemon pepper**
¼ **teaspoon ground ginger**
½ **pound broccoli, coarsely chopped**
1 **red bell pepper, chopped**
1 **can (8 ounces) sliced water chestnuts, drained**
1 **cup baby carrots**
3 **cloves garlic, minced**
1 **jar (16 ounces) Alfredo sauce**
1 **package (8 ounces) wide egg noodles, cooked and drained**

Slow Cooker Directions

1. Combine chicken, onion, chives, basil, olive oil, lemon pepper and ginger in slow cooker; stir thoroughly. Add broccoli, bell pepper, water chestnuts, carrots and garlic; mix well.

2. Cover; cook on LOW 8 hours or on HIGH 4 hours.

3. Add Alfredo sauce; cook on HIGH an additional 30 minutes or until heated through. Serve over hot cooked egg noodles.   *Makes 6 servings*

Easy Chicken Alfredo

Bayou-Style Pot Pie

        1 tablespoon olive oil
        1 large onion, chopped
        1 green bell pepper, chopped
    1½ teaspoons minced garlic
        8 ounces boneless skinless chicken thighs, cut into 1-inch pieces
        1 can (14½ ounces) stewed tomatoes, undrained
        8 ounces fully cooked smoked sausage or kielbasa, thinly sliced
      ¾ teaspoon hot pepper sauce or to taste
    2¼ cups buttermilk baking mix
      ¾ teaspoon dried thyme leaves
      ⅛ teaspoon black pepper
      ⅔ cup milk

1. Preheat oven to 450°F. Heat oil in medium ovenproof skillet over medium-high heat until hot. Add onion, bell pepper and garlic. Cook 3 minutes, stirring occasionally.

2. Add chicken and cook 1 minute. Add tomatoes with juice, sausage and hot pepper sauce. Cook, uncovered, over medium-low heat 5 minutes.

3. While chicken is cooking, combine baking mix, thyme and black pepper. Stir in milk. Drop batter by heaping tablespoonfuls in mounds over chicken mixture. Bake 14 minutes or until biscuits are golden brown and cooked through and chicken mixture is bubbly. *Makes 4 servings*

Note: You can use any of a variety of fully cooked sausages from your supermarket meat case. Andouille, a fairly spicy Louisiana-style sausage, is perfect for this dish.

Prep and Cook Time: 28 minutes

Homestyle Skillet Chicken

    1 tablespoon Cajun seasoning blend
 ½ teaspoon plus ⅛ teaspoon black pepper, divided
 ½ teaspoon salt, divided
    4 chicken thighs
    2 tablespoons vegetable oil
    4 cloves garlic, minced
 ¾ pound small red or new potatoes (about 8), quartered
 12 pearl onions, peeled*
    1 cup peeled baby carrots
    2 ribs celery, halved lengthwise and sliced diagonally into ½-inch
        pieces
 ½ red bell pepper, diced
    2 tablespoons all-purpose flour
    1 cup canned reduced-sodium chicken broth
 ½ cup sherry
    2 tablespoons finely chopped fresh parsley

*To peel pearl onions, drop in boiling water for 30 seconds and plunge immediately into ice water. The peel should slide right off.

1. Combine Cajun seasoning, ½ teaspoon pepper and ¼ teaspoon salt in small bowl. Rub mixture on all sides of chicken.

2. Heat oil in large heavy skillet over medium-high heat. Add garlic and chicken; cook until chicken is browned, about 3 minutes per side. Transfer chicken to plate; set aside.

3. Add potatoes, onions, carrots, celery and bell pepper to skillet. Cook and stir 3 minutes. Sprinkle flour over vegetables; stir to coat. Slowly stir in chicken broth and sherry, scraping up browned bits from bottom of skillet. Bring mixture to a boil, stirring constantly.

4. Reduce heat to medium-low. Return chicken to skillet. Cover and cook about 30 minutes or until juices of chicken run clear. Increase heat to medium-high; cook, uncovered, about 5 minutes or until sauce is thickened. Season with remaining ¼ teaspoon salt and ⅛ teaspoon pepper. Sprinkle with parsley before serving.

Makes 4 servings

Easy Chicken Chalupas

1 roasted chicken (about 2 pounds)
8 flour tortillas
2 cups reduced-fat shredded Cheddar cheese
1 cup mild green chili salsa
1 cup mild red salsa

1. Preheat oven to 350°F. Spray 13×9 ovenproof dish with cooking spray.

2. Remove skin and bones from chicken; discard. Shred chicken meat.

3. Place 2 tortillas in bottom of prepared dish, overlapping slightly. Layer tortillas with 1 cup chicken, ½ cup cheese and ¼ cup of each salsa. Repeat layers, ending with cheese and salsas.

4. Bake casserole 25 minutes or until bubbly and hot.   *Makes 6 servings*

Tip: Serve this easy main dish with some custom toppings on the side such as sour cream, chopped cilantro, sliced black olives, sliced green onions and sliced avocado.

Easy Chicken Chalupas

Chicken Normandy Style

2 tablespoons butter, divided
3 cups peeled, thinly sliced apples, such as Fuji or Braeburn (about
**   3 apples)**
1 pound ground chicken
¼ cup apple brandy or apple juice
1 can (10¾ ounces) condensed cream of chicken soup, undiluted
¼ cup finely chopped green onions (green part only)
2 teaspoons fresh minced sage *or* ½ teaspoon dried sage leaves
¼ teaspoon black pepper
1 package (12 ounces) egg noodles, cooked and drained

1. Preheat oven to 350°F. Grease 9-inch square casserole dish.

2. Melt 1 tablespoon butter in 12-inch nonstick skillet. Add apple slices; cook and stir over medium heat 7 to 10 minutes or until tender. Remove apple slices from skillet.

3. Add ground chicken to same skillet; cook and stir over medium heat until brown, breaking up with spoon. Stir in apple brandy and cook 2 minutes. Stir in soup, green onions, sage, pepper and apple slices. Simmer 5 minutes.

4. Toss noodles with remaining 1 tablespoon butter. Spoon into prepared casserole. Top with chicken mixture. Bake 15 minutes or until hot.   *Makes 4 servings*

Note: Ground turkey, ground pork or tofu crumbles can be substituted for chicken, if desired.

Chicken Normandy Style

Italian Chicken with Sausage and Peppers

2½ pounds chicken pieces
2 tablespoons olive oil
½ to ¾ pounds sweet Italian sausage
2 green bell peppers, chopped
1 onion, chopped
1 carrot, finely chopped
2 cloves garlic, minced
1 can (15 ounces) tomato sauce
1 can (19 ounces) condensed tomato soup, undiluted
¼ teaspoon dried oregano
¼ teaspoon dried basil
1 bay leaf
Salt and pepper

Slow Cooker Directions

1. Rinse chicken; pat dry. Heat oil in large skillet over medium-high heat. Add chicken, skin side down. Cook about 10 minutes, turning to brown both sides. Remove and reserve.

2. Add sausage to skillet and cook 4 to 5 minutes or until browned. Remove, cut into 1-inch pieces and reserve. Drain off all but 1 tablespoon fat from skillet.

3. Add bell peppers, onion, carrot and garlic to skillet. Cook 4 to 5 minutes or until vegetables are tender.

4. Add tomato sauce, tomato soup, oregano, basil and bay leaf; stir well. Season with salt and pepper. Transfer to slow cooker.

5. Add chicken and sausage to slow cooker. Cover; cook on LOW 6 to 8 hours or on HIGH 4 to 6 hours. Remove and discard bay leaf before serving.

Makes 6 servings

Italian Chicken with Sausage and Peppers

Peerless Pork

Pork Chops and Apple Stuffing Bake

  6 (¾-inch-thick) boneless pork loin chops (about 1½ pounds)
  ¼ teaspoon salt
  ⅛ teaspoon black pepper
  1 tablespoon vegetable oil
  1 small onion, chopped
  2 ribs celery, chopped
  2 Granny Smith apples, peeled and coarsely chopped (about
     2 cups)
  1 can (14½ ounces) reduced-sodium chicken broth
  1 can (10¾ ounces) condensed cream of celery soup, undiluted
  ¼ cup dry white wine
  6 cups herb-seasoned stuffing cubes

1. Preheat oven to 375°F. Spray 13×9-inch baking dish with nonstick cooking spray.

2. Season both sides of pork chops with salt and pepper. Heat oil in large deep skillet over medium-high heat until hot. Add chops and cook until browned on both sides, turning once. Remove chops from skillet; set aside.

3. Add onion and celery to same skillet. Cook and stir 3 minutes or until onion is tender. Add apples; cook and stir 1 minute. Add broth, soup and wine; mix well. Bring to a simmer; remove from heat. Stir in stuffing cubes until evenly moistened.

4. Spread stuffing mixture evenly in prepared dish. Place pork chops on top of stuffing; pour any accumulated juices over chops. Cover tightly with foil and bake 30 to 40 minutes or until pork chops are juicy and barely pink in center.

Makes 6 servings

Pork Chops and Apple Stuffing Bake

Cajun-Style Country Ribs

2 cups baby carrots
1 large onion, coarsely chopped
1 large green bell pepper, cut into 1-inch pieces
1 large red bell pepper, cut into 1-inch pieces
2 teaspoons minced fresh garlic
2 tablespoons Cajun or Creole seasoning mix, divided
3½ to 4 pounds country-style pork spareribs
1 can (14½ ounces) stewed tomatoes, undrained
2 tablespoons water
1 tablespoon cornstarch
Hot cooked rice

Slow Cooker Directions

1. Place carrots, onion, bell peppers, garlic and 2 teaspoons seasoning mix in slow cooker; mix well.

2. Trim excess fat from ribs. Cut into individual riblets. Sprinkle 1 tablespoon seasoning mix over ribs; place in slow cooker over vegetables. Pour tomatoes with juice over ribs (slow cooker will be full). Cover; cook on LOW 6 to 8 hours or until ribs are fork tender.

3. Remove ribs and vegetables from cooking liquid to serving platter. Let liquid stand 5 minutes to allow fat to rise. Skim off fat. Blend water, cornstarch and remaining 1 teaspoon Cajun seasoning. Stir into liquid in slow cooker. Cook on HIGH until sauce is thickened. Return ribs and vegetables to sauce; carefully stirring to coat. Serve with rice. *Makes 6 servings*

Prep Time: 15 minutes
Cook Time: 6 to 8 hours

Cajun-Style Country Ribs

Easy Moroccan Casserole

2 tablespoons vegetable oil
1 pound pork stew meat, cut into 1-inch cubes
½ cup chopped onion
3 tablespoons all-purpose flour
1 can (about 14 ounces) diced tomatoes, undrained
¼ cup water
1 teaspoon ground ginger
1 teaspoon ground cumin
1 teaspoon ground cinnamon
½ teaspoon sugar
½ teaspoon salt
½ teaspoon black pepper
2 medium unpeeled red potatoes, cut into ½-inch pieces
1 large sweet potato, peeled and cut into ½-inch pieces
1 cup frozen lima beans, thawed and drained
1 cup frozen cut green beans, thawed and drained
¾ cup sliced carrots
Pita bread

1. Preheat oven to 325°F.

2. Heat oil in large skillet over medium-high heat. Add pork and onion; cook until pork is browned on all sides, stirring occasionally. Sprinkle flour over meat mixture. Stir until flour has absorbed pan juices. Cook 2 minutes more.

3. Stir in tomatoes with juice, water, ginger, cumin, cinnamon, sugar, salt and pepper. Transfer mixture to 2-quart casserole. Bake 30 minutes.

4. Stir in red potatoes, sweet potato, lima beans, green beans and carrots. Cover; bake 1 hour or until potatoes are tender. Serve with warm pita bread.

Makes 6 servings

Easy Moroccan Casserole

Sweet Kraut Chops

3 pounds bone-in pork rib chops
½ teaspoon garlic powder
½ teaspoon black pepper
1 bag (32 ounces) sauerkraut
1 cup applesauce

Slow Cooker Directions

1. Place pork chops in slow cooker. Sprinkle with garlic powder and pepper. Pour sauerkraut, then applesauce over pork.

2. Cover; cook on LOW 6 to 8 hours or until pork is tender.

Makes 6 to 8 servings

Panama Pork Stew

2 small sweet potatoes (about 12 ounces), peeled and cut into
** 2-inch pieces**
1 package (10 ounces) frozen corn
1 package (9 ounces) frozen cut green beans
1 cup chopped onion
1¼ pounds lean pork stew meat, cut into 1-inch cubes
1 can (14½ ounces) diced tomatoes, undrained
¼ cup water
1 to 2 tablespoons chili powder
½ teaspoon salt
½ teaspoon ground coriander

Slow Cooker Directions

1. Place potatoes, corn, green beans and onion in slow cooker. Top with pork.

2. Combine tomatoes with juice, water, chili powder, salt and coriander in medium bowl. Pour over pork in slow cooker.

3. Cover; cook on LOW 7 to 9 hours.

Makes 6 servings

Pork Chops with Jalapeño-Pecan Cornbread Stuffing

        6 boneless loin pork chops, 1 inch thick (1½ pounds)
          Nonstick cooking spray
    ¾ cup chopped onion
    ¾ cup chopped celery
    ½ cup coarsely chopped pecans
    ½ medium jalapeño pepper,* seeded and chopped
      1 teaspoon rubbed sage
    ½ teaspoon dried rosemary
    ⅛ teaspoon black pepper
      4 cups unseasoned cornbread stuffing mix
  1¼ cups reduced-sodium chicken broth
      1 egg, lightly beaten

*Jalapeño peppers can sting and irritate the skin; wear rubber gloves when handling peppers and do not touch eyes. Wash hands after handling.

Slow Cooker Directions

1. Trim excess fat from pork and discard. Spray large skillet with nonstick cooking spray; heat over medium heat. Add pork; cook 10 minutes or until browned on both sides. Remove; set aside. Add onion, celery, pecans, jalapeño pepper, sage, rosemary and pepper to skillet. Cook 5 minutes or until onion and celery are tender; set aside.

2. Combine cornbread stuffing mix, vegetable mixture and broth in medium bowl. Stir in egg. Spoon stuffing mixture into slow cooker. Arrange pork on top. Cover and cook on LOW about 5 hours or until pork is tender and barely pink in center. Serve with vegetable salad, if desired.   *Makes 6 servings*

Note: If you prefer a more moist dressing, increase the chicken broth to 1½ cups.

Shredded Pork Wraps

1 cup salsa, divided
2 tablespoons cornstarch
1 bone-in pork sirloin roast (2 pounds)
6 (8-inch) flour tortillas
3 cups broccoli slaw mix
⅓ cup shredded reduced-fat Cheddar cheese

Slow Cooker Directions

1. Combine ¼ cup salsa and cornstarch in small bowl; stir until smooth. Pour mixture into slow cooker. Top with pork roast. Pour remaining ¾ cup salsa over roast.

2. Cover; cook on LOW 6 to 8 hours or until internal temperature reaches 165°F when tested with meat thermometer inserted into thickest part of roast, not touching bone. Transfer roast to cutting board; cover with foil and let stand 10 to 15 minutes or until cool enough to handle. (Internal temperature will rise 5° to 10°F during stand time.) Trim and discard outer fat from pork. Using 2 forks, pull pork into coarse shreds.

3. Divide shredded meat evenly among tortillas. Spoon about 2 tablespoons salsa mixture on top of meat in each tortilla. Top evenly with broccoli slaw and cheese. Fold bottom edge of tortilla over filling; fold in sides. Roll up completely to enclose filling. Serve remaining salsa mixture as dipping sauce. *Makes 6 servings*

Shredded Pork Wrap

Sweet 'n' Spicy Ribs

5 cups barbecue sauce*
¾ cup brown sugar
¼ cup honey
2 tablespoons Cajun seasoning
1 tablespoon garlic powder
1 tablespoon onion powder
6 pounds pork or beef back ribs, cut into 3-rib portions

Barbecue sauce adds a significant flavor to this recipe. Use your favorite sauce to ensure you fully enjoy the dish.

Slow Cooker Directions

1. Stir together barbecue sauce, brown sugar, honey, Cajun seasoning, garlic powder and onion powder in medium bowl. Remove 1 cup mixture; refrigerate and reserve for dipping sauce.

2. Place ribs in large slow cooker. Pour barbecue sauce mixture over ribs. Cover; cook on LOW 8 hours or until meat is very tender.

3. Uncover; remove ribs. Skim fat from sauce. Serve with reserved sauce.

Makes 10 servings

Cook's Comment: This dish is excellent over rice.

Sweet 'n' Spicy Ribs

Carolina Baked Beans & Pork Chops

2 cans (16 ounces each) pork and beans
½ cup chopped onion
½ cup chopped green bell pepper
¼ cup *French's® Classic Yellow®* Mustard
¼ cup packed light brown sugar
2 tablespoons *French's®* Worcestershire Sauce
1 tablespoon *Frank's® RedHot®* Original Cayenne Pepper Sauce
6 boneless pork chops (1 inch thick)

1. Preheat oven to 400°F. Combine all ingredients *except pork chops* in 3-quart shallow baking dish; mix well. Arrange chops on top, turning once to coat with sauce.

2. Bake uncovered 30 to 35 minutes or until pork is no longer pink in center. Stir beans around chops once during baking. Serve with green beans or mashed potatoes, if desired. *Makes 6 servings*

Prep Time: 10 minutes
Cook Time: 30 minutes

Glazed Pork Loin

1 bag (1 pound) baby carrots
4 boneless pork loin chops
1 jar (8 ounces) apricot preserves

Slow Cooker Directions

1. Place carrots in bottom of slow cooker. Place pork on carrots and brush with preserves.

2. Cover; cook on LOW 8 hours or on HIGH 4 hours. *Makes 4 servings*

Carolina Baked Beans & Pork Chop

Old-Fashioned Cabbage Rolls

½ **pound ground beef**
½ **pound ground veal**
½ **pound ground pork**
 1 **small onion, chopped**
 2 **eggs, lightly beaten**
½ **cup dry bread crumbs**
 1 **teaspoon salt**
 1 **teaspoon molasses**
¼ **teaspoon ground ginger**
¼ **teaspoon ground nutmeg**
¼ **teaspoon ground allspice**
 1 **large head cabbage, separated into leaves**
 3 **cups boiling water**
¼ **cup butter or margarine**
½ **cup milk, or more as needed**
 1 **tablespoon cornstarch**

1. Combine meats and onion in large bowl. Combine eggs, bread crumbs, salt, molasses, ginger, nutmeg and allspice in medium bowl; mix well. Add to meat mixture and mix well.

2. Drop cabbage leaves into boiling water for 3 minutes. Remove with slotted spoon, reserving ½ cup of boiling liquid.

3. Preheat oven to 375°F. Place about 2 tablespoons meat mixture about 1 inch from stem end of each leaf. Fold sides in and roll up, fastening with toothpicks, if necessary.

4. Heat butter in large skillet over medium-high heat. Add cabbage rolls (3 or 4 at a time) to skillet and brown on all sides. Arrange rolls, seam side down, in single layer in casserole. Combine reserved boiling liquid with butter remaining in skillet; pour over cabbage rolls.

5. Bake 1 hour. Remove and carefully drain accumulated pan juices into measuring cup. Return cabbage rolls to oven. Add enough milk to pan juices to equal 1 cup.

6. Pour milk mixture into small saucepan; stir in cornstarch and bring to a boil, stirring constantly until sauce is thickened. Pour over cabbage rolls. Bake 15 minutes more or until sauce is browned and cabbage is very tender.   *Makes 8 serving*

Mexi-Tortilla Casserole

1 tablespoon vegetable oil
1 small onion, chopped
1 pound ground pork*
1 can (14½ ounces) diced tomatoes, undrained
1 teaspoon dried oregano
¼ teaspoon salt
¼ teaspoon ground cumin
¼ teaspoon pepper
1½ cups (6 ounces) shredded pepper-Jack or taco-flavored cheese
2 cups tortilla chips
½ cup reduced-fat sour cream
1 can (4 ounces) diced green chilies, drained
2 tablespoons minced cilantro

*For a vegetarian casserole, substitute 1 pound tofu crumbles for the pork.

1. Preheat oven to 350°F.

2. Heat oil in large skillet. Add onion and cook 5 minutes or until tender. Add pork and cook until brown, stirring to separate meat. Pour off fat. Stir in tomatoes with juice, oregano, salt, cumin and pepper. Spoon into 11×7-inch casserole. Sprinkle cheese over casserole; arrange tortilla chips over cheese. Bake 10 to 15 minutes or until cheese melts.

3. Combine sour cream and chilies; mix until well blended. Drop by tablespoonfuls over baked casserole. Sprinkle with cilantro.   *Makes 6 servings*

Pork with Savory Apple Stuffing

1 package (6 ounces) corn bread stuffing mix
1 can (14½ ounces) chicken broth
1 small apple, peeled, cored and chopped
¼ cup chopped celery
1⅓ cups *French's®* **French Fried Onions, divided**
4 boneless pork chops, ¾ inch thick (about 1 pound)
½ cup peach-apricot sweet & sour sauce
1 tablespoon *French's®* **Honey Dijon Mustard**

1. Preheat oven to 375°F. Combine stuffing mix, broth, apple, celery and ⅔ *cup* French Fried Onions in large bowl. Spoon into bottom of greased shallow 2-quart baking dish. Arrange chops on top of stuffing.

2. Combine sweet & sour sauce with mustard in small bowl. Pour over pork. Bake 40 minutes or until pork is no longer pink in center.

3. Sprinkle with remaining onions. Bake 5 minutes or until onions are golden.

Makes 4 servings

Prep Time: 10 minutes
Cook Time: 45 minutes

Pork with Savory Apple Stuffing

Spicy Asian Pork Filling

1 boneless pork sirloin roast (about 3 pounds)
½ cup tamari or soy sauce
1 tablespoon chili garlic sauce or chili paste
2 teaspoons minced fresh ginger
2 tablespoons water
1 tablespoon cornstarch
2 teaspoons dark sesame oil

Slow Cooker Directions

1. Cut roast into 2- to 3-inch chunks. Combine pork, tamari sauce, chili garlic sauce and ginger in slow cooker; mix well. Cover; cook on LOW 8 to 10 hours or until pork is fork tender.

2. Remove roast from cooking liquid; cool slightly. Trim and discard excess fat. Shred pork using 2 forks. Let liquid stand 5 minutes to allow fat to rise. Skim off fat.

3. Blend water, cornstarch and sesame oil; whisk into liquid. Cook on HIGH until thickened. Add shredded meat to slow cooker; mix well. Cook 15 to 30 minutes or until hot. *Makes 5½ cups filling*

Spicy Asian Pork Bundles: Place ¼ cup pork filling into large lettuce leaves. Wrap to enclose. Makes about 20 bundles.

Moo Shu Pork: Lightly spread plum sauce over warm small flour tortillas. Spoon ¼ cup pork filling and ¼ cup stir-fried vegetables into flour tortillas. Wrap to enclose. Serve immediately. Makes enough to fill about 20 tortillas.

Prep Time: 15 to 20 minutes
Cook Time: 8 to 10 hours

Spicy Asian Pork Filling

Honey Ribs

1 can (10¾ ounces) condensed beef consommé, undiluted
½ cup water
3 tablespoons soy sauce
2 tablespoons honey
2 tablespoons maple syrup
2 tablespoons barbecue sauce
½ teaspoon dry mustard
2 pounds pork baby back ribs, trimmed

Slow Cooker Directions

1. Combine all ingredients except ribs in slow cooker; mix well.

2. Cut ribs into 3- to 4-rib portions. Add ribs to slow cooker. (If ribs are especially fatty, broil 10 minutes before adding to slow cooker.)

3. Cover; cook on LOW 6 to 8 hours or on HIGH 4 to 6 hours or until ribs are tender. Cut into individual ribs. Serve with sauce. *Makes 4 servings*

Honey Ribs

Pork Roast Landaise

  2 tablespoons olive oil
2½ pounds boneless center cut pork loin roast
    Salt and pepper
  1 medium sweet onion, diced
  2 large cloves garlic, minced
  2 teaspoons dried thyme
  2 cups chicken stock, divided
  2 tablespoons cornstarch or arrowroot
  ¼ cup red wine vinegar
  ¼ cup sugar
  ½ cup port or sherry wine
  2 parsnips, cut in ¾-inch slices
1½ cups pitted prunes
  3 pears, cored and sliced ¾-inch thick

Slow Cooker Directions

1. Heat olive oil in large saucepan over medium-high heat. Season pork roast with salt and pepper and brown in saucepan on all sides. Remove browned roast from pan and place in slow cooker.

2. Add onion and garlic to saucepan. Cook and stir over medium heat for 2 to 3 minutes. Stir in thyme. Add onion mixture to slow cooker.

3. In small bowl, mix ¼ cup of chicken stock with the cornstarch; set aside.

4. Combine vinegar and sugar in same saucepan in which onion and garlic were cooked. Cook over medium heat, stirring constantly, until mixture thickens into syrup. Add port and cook 1 minute more. Add remaining 1¾ cups chicken stock. Whisk in cornstarch mixture and cook until smooth and slightly thickened. Pour into slow cooker.

5. Cover; cook on LOW 8 hours or on HIGH 4 hours. During the last 30 minutes of cooking, add parsnips, prunes and pears. Serve over rice or mashed potatoes or with French bread to dunk in the gravy, if desired. *Makes 4 to 6 servings*

Pork Roast Landaise

Hungarian Goulash Casserole

1 pound ground pork
¼ teaspoon salt
¼ teaspoon ground nutmeg
¼ teaspoon black pepper
1 tablespoon vegetable oil
1 cup reduced-fat sour cream, divided
1 tablespoon cornstarch
1 can (10¾ ounces) condensed cream of celery soup, undiluted
1 cup milk
1 teaspoon sweet Hungarian paprika
1 package (12 ounces) egg noodles, cooked and drained
2 teaspoons minced fresh dill (optional)

1. Preheat oven to 325°F. Spray 13×9-inch casserole dish with nonstick cooking spray.

2. Combine pork, salt, nutmeg and pepper in bowl. Shape into 1-inch meatballs. Heat oil in large skillet over medium-high heat. Add meatballs. Cook 10 minutes or until browned on all sides and no longer pink in centers. Remove meatballs from skillet; discard drippings.

3. Stir together ¼ cup sour cream and cornstarch in small bowl. Spoon into same skillet. Add remaining ¾ cup sour cream, soup, milk and paprika. Stir until smooth.

4. Spoon cooked noodles into prepared dish. Arrange meatballs over noodles and cover with sauce. Bake 20 minutes or until hot. Sprinkle with dill, if desired.

Make 4 to 6 servings

Hungarian Goulash Casserole

Shredded Apricot Pork Sandwiches

    2 medium onions, thinly sliced
    1 cup apricot preserves
    ½ cup barbecue sauce
    ½ cup packed dark brown sugar
    ¼ cup cider vinegar
    2 tablespoons Worcestershire sauce
    ½ teaspoon red pepper flakes
    1 (4-pound) boneless pork loin roast, trimmed of fat
    ¼ cup cold water
    2 tablespoons cornstarch
    1 tablespoon grated fresh ginger
    1 teaspoon salt
    1 teaspoon black pepper
    10 to 12 sesame or onion rolls, toasted

Slow Cooker Directions

1. Combine onions, preserves, barbecue sauce, brown sugar, vinegar, Worcestershire sauce and pepper flakes in small bowl. Place pork roast in slow cooker. Pour apricot mixture over roast. Cover; cook on LOW 8 to 9 hours.

2. Remove pork from cooking liquid to cutting board; cool slightly. Using 2 forks, shred pork into coarse shreds. Let liquid stand 5 minutes to allow fat to rise. Skim fat.

3. Combine water, cornstarch, ginger, salt and pepper; blend well. Whisk cornstarch mixture into slow cooker liquid. Cook on HIGH 15 to 30 minutes or until thickened. Return shredded pork to slow cooker; mix well. Serve in toasted buns.

Makes 10 to 12 sandwiches

Variation: One (4-pound) pork shoulder roast, cut into pieces and trimmed of fat, can be substituted for pork loin roast.

Pork & Rice Provençal

4 well-trimmed boneless pork loin chops, ¾-inch thick (about 1 pound)
1 teaspoon dried basil
½ teaspoon dried thyme
½ teaspoon garlic salt
¼ teaspoon ground black pepper
2 tablespoons margarine or butter, divided
1 (6.8-ounce) package RICE-A-RONI® Beef Flavor
½ cup chopped onion
1 clove garlic, minced
1 (14½-ounce) can seasoned diced tomatoes, undrained
1 (2¼-ounce) can sliced ripe olives, drained or ⅓ cup sliced pitted kalamata olives

1. Sprinkle pork chops with basil, thyme, garlic salt and pepper; set aside. In large skillet over medium-high heat, melt 1 tablespoon margarine. Add pork chops; cook 3 minutes. Reduce heat to medium; turn pork chops over and cook 3 minutes. Remove from skillet; set aside.

2. In same skillet over medium heat, sauté rice-vermicelli mix, onion and garlic with remaining 1 tablespoon margarine until vermicelli is golden brown.

3. Slowly stir in 1¾ cups water, tomatoes and Special Seasonings; bring to a boil. Cover; reduce heat to low. Simmer 10 minutes.

4. Add pork chops and olives. Cover; simmer 10 minutes or until rice is tender and pork chops are no longer pink inside.   *Makes 4 servings*

Prep Time: 10 minutes
Cook Time: 40 minutes

Cheesy Pork and Potatoes

½ **pound ground pork, cooked and crumbled**
½ **cup finely crushed saltine crackers**
⅓ **cup barbecue sauce**
1 **egg**
3 **tablespoons margarine**
1 **tablespoon vegetable oil**
4 **potatoes, peeled and thinly sliced**
1 **onion, thinly sliced**
1 **cup grated mozzarella cheese**
⅔ **cup evaporated milk**
1 **teaspoon salt**
¼ **teaspoon paprika**
⅛ **teaspoon black pepper**
Chopped fresh parsley

Slow Cooker Directions

1. Combine pork, crackers, barbecue sauce and egg in large bowl; shape mixture into 6 patties. Heat margarine and oil in medium skillet. Sauté potatoes and onion until lightly browned. Drain and place in slow cooker.

2. Combine cheese, milk, salt, paprika and pepper in small bowl. Pour into slow cooker. Layer pork patties on top.

3. Cover; cook on LOW 3 to 5 hours. Garnish with parsley. *Makes 6 servings*

Cheesy Pork and Potatoes

Potato and Pork Frittata

12 ounces (about 3 cups) frozen hash brown potatoes
1 teaspoon Cajun seasoning
4 egg whites
2 whole eggs
¼ cup low-fat (1%) milk
1 teaspoon dry mustard
¼ teaspoon black pepper
10 ounces (about 3 cups) frozen stir-fry vegetable blend
⅓ cup water
¾ cup chopped cooked lean pork
½ cup (2 ounces) shredded Cheddar cheese

1. Preheat oven to 400°F. Spray baking sheet with nonstick cooking spray. Spread potatoes on baking sheet; sprinkle with Cajun seasoning. Bake 15 minutes or until hot. Remove from oven. *Reduce oven temperature to 350°F.*

2. Beat egg whites, eggs, milk, mustard and pepper in small bowl. Place vegetables and water in medium ovenproof nonstick skillet. Cook over medium heat 5 minutes or until vegetables are crisp-tender; drain.

3. Add pork and potatoes to vegetables in skillet; stir lightly. Add egg mixture. Sprinkle with cheese. Cook over medium-low heat 5 minutes. Place skillet in 350°F oven and bake 5 minutes or until egg mixture is set and cheese is melted.

Makes 4 servings

Prep and Cook Time: 30 minutes

Potato and Pork Frittata

Barbecued Pulled Pork

1 boneless pork shoulder or butt roast (3 to 4 pounds)
1 teaspoon salt
1 teaspoon ground cumin
1 teaspoon paprika
1 teaspoon black pepper
½ teaspoon ground red pepper
1 medium onion, thinly sliced
1 medium green bell pepper, cut into strips
1 bottle (18 ounces) barbecue sauce
½ cup packed light brown sugar
Sandwich rolls
Hot cooked rice
Flour tortillas

Slow Cooker Directions

1. Trim excess fat from pork. Combine salt, cumin, paprika, black pepper and red pepper in small bowl; rub over roast.

2. Place onion and bell pepper in slow cooker; add pork. Combine barbecue sauce and brown sugar in medium bowl; pour over meat. Cover; cook on LOW 8 to 10 hours.

3. Transfer roast to cutting board. Trim and discard fat from roast. Using 2 forks, pull pork into coarse shreds. Serve pork with sauce on sandwich rolls or over rice with tortillas.   *Makes 4 to 6 servings*

Barbecued Pulled Pork

Cantonese Pork

2 pork tenderloins (about 2 pounds)
1 tablespoon vegetable oil
1 can (8 ounces) pineapple chunks in juice, undrained
1 can (8 ounces) tomato sauce
2 cans (4 ounces each) sliced mushrooms, drained
1 medium onion, thinly sliced
3 tablespoons brown sugar
2 tablespoons Worcestershire sauce
1½ teaspoons salt
1½ teaspoons white vinegar
Hot cooked rice

Slow Cooker Directions

1. Cut tenderloins in half lengthwise, then crosswise into ¼-inch slices. Heat oil in large nonstick skillet over medium-low heat. Brown pork on all sides. Drain excess fat; discard.

2. Place pork, pineapple with juice, tomato sauce, mushrooms, onions, sugar, Worcestershire, salt and vinegar in slow cooker.

3. Cover; cook on LOW 6 to 8 hours or on HIGH 4 hours. Serve over rice.

Makes 8 servings

Cantonese Pork

Pork Meatballs & Sauerkraut

1 ¼ pounds lean ground pork
¾ cup dry bread crumbs
1 egg, lightly beaten
2 tablespoons milk
2 teaspoons caraway seeds, divided
1 teaspoon salt
½ teaspoon Worcestershire sauce
¼ teaspoon black pepper
1 bag (32 ounces) sauerkraut, drained, squeezed dry and snipped
½ cup chopped onion
6 slices bacon, crisp-cooked and crumbled
Chopped parsley

Slow Cooker Directions

1. Combine ground pork, bread crumbs, egg, milk, 1 teaspoon caraway seeds, salt, Worcestershire and pepper in large bowl. Shape mixture into 2-inch balls. Brown meatballs in large nonstick skillet over medium-high heat.

2. Combine sauerkraut, onion, bacon and remaining 1 teaspoon caraway seeds in slow cooker. Place meatballs on top of sauerkraut mixture.

3. Cover; cook on LOW 6 to 8 hours. Garnish with chopped parsley.

Makes 4 to 6 servings

Prep Time: 30 minutes
Cook Time: 6 to 8 hours

Pork Meatballs & Sauerkraut

Simply Delicious Pork

1½ **pounds boneless pork loin, cut into 6 pieces** *or* **6 boneless pork loin chops**
 4 **medium Yellow Delicious apples, sliced**
 3 **tablespoons brown sugar**
 1 **teaspoon ground cinnamon**
 ½ **teaspoon salt**

Slow Cooker Directions

1. Place pork in slow cooker. Cover with apples.

2. Combine brown sugar, cinnamon and salt in small bowl; sprinkle over apples. Cover; cook on LOW 6 to 8 hours. *Makes 6 servings*

Ale'd Pork and Sauerkraut

 1 **jar (32 ounces) sauerkraut, undrained**
1½ **tablespoons sugar**
 1 **can (12 ounces) dark beer or ale**
3½ **pounds boneless pork shoulder or pork butt roast**
 ½ **teaspoon salt**
 ¼ **teaspoon garlic powder**
 ¼ **teaspoon black pepper**
 Paprika

Slow Cooker Directions

1. Place sauerkraut into slow cooker. Sprinkle sugar evenly over sauerkraut; pour beer over all. Place pork, fat side up, on top of sauerkraut mixture; sprinkle evenly with remaining ingredients.

2. Cover; cook on HIGH 6 hours.

3. Remove pork to serving platter. Remove sauerkraut with slotted spoon; arrange around pork. Spoon about ½ to ¾ cup cooking liquid over sauerkraut, if desired. *Makes 6 to 8 servings*

City Chicken BBQ Casserole

2 tablespoons vegetable oil
6 to 8 boneless pork chops (about 2 pounds), cut into bite-size
    pieces
¼ cup chopped onions
2 cloves garlic, chopped
2 cups water
2 cups uncooked instant white rice
2 cups (8 ounces) shredded mozzarella cheese

Sauce
1 bottle (12 ounces) chili sauce
1 cup ketchup
½ cup packed brown sugar
2 tablespoons honey
1 tablespoon Worcestershire sauce
1 tablespoon hot pepper jelly
1 teaspoon ground ginger
1 teaspoon liquid smoke (optional)
½ teaspoon curry powder
¼ teaspoon black pepper

1. Preheat oven to 350°F.

2. Heat oil in large skillet over medium-high heat until hot. Add pork; cook and stir 10 to 15 minutes or until browned and barely pink in center. Add onions and garlic; cook until onions are tender. Drain fat.

3. Meanwhile, bring water to a boil in small saucepan. Stir in rice; cover. Remove from heat; let stand 5 minutes or until water is absorbed.

4. Combine sauce ingredients in separate saucepan; bring to a boil. Reduce heat to low; cover and simmer 10 minutes, stirring occasionally.

5. Combine pork mixture, rice and sauce in 2½-quart casserole; mix well. Bake 15 to 20 minutes. Top with mozzarella cheese and bake 5 minutes more. Serve hot.

Makes 6 to 8 servings

Note: "City chicken" is a traditional dish in Ohio and Pennsylvania. The name indicates that chicken was once more expensive than pork, so the cheaper pork cuts were prepared to taste like chicken.

Mexican Skillet Rice

¾ pound lean ground pork or lean ground beef
1 medium onion, chopped
1½ tablespoons chili powder
1 teaspoon ground cumin
½ teaspoon salt
3 cups cooked brown rice
1 can (16 ounces) pinto beans, drained
2 cans (4 ounces each) diced green chilies
1 medium tomato, seeded and chopped (optional)

Cook meat in large skillet over medium-high heat until brown, stirring to crumble; drain. Return meat to skillet. Add onion, chili powder, cumin and salt; cook until onion is soft but not brown. Stir in rice, beans and chilies; heat through. Top with tomato.

Makes 6 servings

Microwave Directions: Combine meat and onion in 2- to 3-quart microwave-safe baking dish, stirring well. Cover with waxed paper and cook on HIGH 4 to 5 minutes, stirring after 2 minutes, or until meat is no longer pink. Drain. Add chili powder, cumin, salt, rice, beans and chiles. Cook on HIGH 4 to 5 minutes, stirring after 2 minutes, or until thoroughly heated. Top with tomato.

Mexican Skillet Rice

Spicy Pork Chop Casserole

Nonstick cooking spray
2 cups frozen corn
2 cups frozen diced hash brown potatoes
1 can (14½ ounces) diced tomatoes with basil, garlic and oregano,
    drained
2 teaspoons chili powder
1 teaspoon dried oregano leaves
½ teaspoon ground cumin
⅛ teaspoon dried red pepper flakes
1 teaspoon olive oil
4 (3-ounce) boneless pork loin chops, cut about ¾ inch thick
¼ teaspoon black pepper
¼ cup (1 ounce) shredded reduced-fat Monterey Jack cheese
    (optional)

1. Preheat oven to 375°F.

2. Lightly spray nonstick skillet with cooking spray. Add corn; cook and stir over medium-high heat about 5 minutes or until corn begins to brown. Add potatoes; cook and stir about 5 minutes more or until potatoes begin to brown. Add tomatoes, chili powder, oregano, cumin and red pepper; stir until blended.

3. Lightly spray 8×8×2-inch baking dish with cooking spray. Transfer corn mixture to prepared dish.

4. Wipe skillet with paper towel. Add oil and pork chops to skillet. Cook pork chops over medium-high heat until brown on one side. Remove pork chops; place, browned side up, on top of corn mixture in baking dish. Sprinkle with black pepper. Bake, uncovered, 20 minutes or until meat is juicy and barely pink in center. Sprinkle with cheese, if desired. Let stand 2 to 3 minutes before serving.   *Makes 4 servings*

Prep Time: 15 minutes
Bake Time: 20 minutes

Spicy Pork Chop Casserole

Stew Provençal

2 cans (about 14 ounces each) beef broth, divided
⅓ cup all-purpose flour
1 to 2 pork tenderloins (about 2 pounds), trimmed and diced
4 red potatoes, unpeeled, cut into cubes
2 cups frozen cut green beans
1 onion, chopped
2 cloves garlic, minced
1 teaspoon salt
1 teaspoon dried thyme leaves
½ teaspoon black pepper

Slow Cooker Directions

1. Combine ¾ cup beef broth and flour in small bowl. Set aside.

2. Add remaining broth, pork, potatoes, beans, onion, garlic, salt, thyme and pepper to slow cooker; stir.

3. Cover and cook on LOW 8 to 10 hours or on HIGH 4 to 5 hours. If cooking on LOW, turn to HIGH last 30 minutes. Stir in flour mixture. Cook 30 minutes to thicken.

Makes 8 servings

Stew Provençal

Simple Shredded Pork Tacos

      2 pounds boneless pork roast
      1 cup salsa
      1 can (4 ounces) diced green chilies
   ½ teaspoon garlic salt
   ½ teaspoon pepper

Slow Cooker Directions

1. Place all ingredients in slow cooker.

2. Cover; cook on LOW 8 hours or until meat is tender. To serve, use 2 forks to shred pork.   *Makes 6 servings*

Sweet & Saucy Ribs

      2 pounds pork baby back ribs
      1 teaspoon black pepper
   2½ cups barbecue sauce (not mesquite flavored)
      1 jar (8 ounces) cherry jam or preserves
      1 tablespoon Dijon mustard
   ¼ teaspoon salt
      Additional salt and black pepper (optional)

Slow Cooker Directions

1. Trim excess fat from ribs. Rub 1 teaspoon black pepper over ribs. Cut ribs into 2-rib portions; place into slow cooker.

2. Combine barbecue sauce, jam, mustard and salt in small bowl; pour over ribs.

3. Cover; cook on LOW 6 to 8 hours or until ribs are tender. Season with additional salt and pepper, if desired. Serve ribs with sauce.   *Makes 4 servings*

Prep Time: 10 minutes
Cook Time: 6 to 8 hours (LOW)

Simple Shredded Pork Tacos

Pork and Mushroom Ragout

1 boneless pork loin roast (1¼ pounds)
1¼ cups canned crushed tomatoes, divided
2 tablespoons cornstarch
2 teaspoons dried savory leaves
3 sun-dried tomatoes, chopped
1 package (8 ounces) sliced mushrooms
1 large onion, sliced
1 teaspoon black pepper
3 cups hot cooked noodles

Slow Cooker Directions

1. Spray large nonstick skillet with nonstick cooking spray; heat skillet over medium heat until hot. Brown roast on all sides; set aside.

2. Place ½ cup crushed tomatoes, cornstarch, savory and sun-dried tomatoes into slow cooker; mix well. Layer mushrooms, onion and pork over tomato mixture.

3. Pour remaining tomatoes over pork; sprinkle with pepper. Cover; cook on LOW 4 to 6 hours or until internal temperature reaches 165°F when tested with meat thermometer inserted into the thickest part of roast.

4. Transfer roast to cutting board; cover with foil. Let stand 10 to 15 minutes. Internal temperature will continue to rise 5°F to 10°F during stand time. Slice roast. Serve with sauce over hot cooked noodles. *Makes 6 servings*

Pork and Mushroom Ragout

Meatless Wonders

Eggplant Parmigiana

2 eggs, beaten
¼ cup milk
   Dash garlic powder
   Dash onion powder
   Dash salt
   Dash black pepper
1 large eggplant, cut into ½-inch-thick slices
½ cup seasoned dry bread crumbs
   Vegetable oil for frying
1 jar (about 26 ounces) spaghetti sauce
4 cups (16 ounces) shredded mozzarella cheese
2½ cups (10 ounces) shredded Swiss cheese
¼ cup grated Parmesan cheese
¼ cup grated Romano cheese

1. Preheat oven to 350°F. Combine eggs, milk, garlic powder, onion powder, salt and pepper in shallow bowl. Dip eggplant into egg mixture; coat in bread crumbs.

2. Add enough oil to large skillet to cover bottom by ¼ inch. Heat over medium-high heat. Brown eggplant in batches on both sides; drain on paper towels. Cover bottom of 13×9-inch baking dish with 2 or 3 tablespoons spaghetti sauce. Layer ½ of eggplant, ½ of mozzarella cheese, ½ of Swiss cheese and ½ of remaining sauce in dish. Repeat layers. Sprinkle with Parmesan and Romano cheeses.

3. Bake 30 minutes or until heated through and cheeses are melted.

Makes 4 servings

Eggplant Parmigiana

Chili with Beans and Corn

**1 (16-ounce) can black-eyed peas or cannellini beans, rinsed and
   drained**
1 (16-ounce) can kidney or navy beans, rinsed and drained
1 (15-ounce) can whole tomatoes, drained and chopped
1 onion, chopped
1 cup frozen corn
1 cup water
½ cup chopped green onions
½ cup tomato paste
¼ cup diced jalapeño peppers*
1 tablespoon chili powder
1 teaspoon ground cumin
1 teaspoon prepared mustard
½ teaspoon dried oregano leaves

**Jalapeño peppers can sting and irritate the skin; wear rubber gloves when handling peppers
and do not touch eyes. Wash hands after handling.*

Slow Cooker Directions

Combine all ingredients in slow cooker. Cover; cook on LOW 8 to 10 hours or on
HIGH 4 to 5 hours. *Makes 6 to 8 servings*

Chili with Beans and Corn

Ravioli with Homemade Tomato Sauce

3 cloves garlic, peeled
½ cup fresh basil leaves
3 cups seeded peeled tomatoes, cut into quarters
2 tablespoons tomato paste
2 tablespoons prepared fat-free Italian salad dressing
1 tablespoon balsamic vinegar
¼ teaspoon black pepper
1 package (9 ounces) uncooked refrigerated reduced-fat cheese ravioli
2 cups shredded washed spinach leaves
1 cup (4 ounces) shredded part-skim mozzarella cheese

Microwave Directions

1. To prepare tomato sauce, process garlic in food processor until coarsely chopped. Add basil; process until coarsely chopped. Add tomatoes, tomato paste, salad dressing, vinegar and pepper; process, using on/off pulsing action, until tomatoes are chopped.

2. Spray 9-inch square microwavable dish with nonstick cooking spray. Spread 1 cup tomato sauce in dish. Layer half of ravioli and spinach over tomato sauce. Repeat layers with 1 cup tomato sauce and remaining ravioli and spinach. Top with remaining 1 cup tomato sauce. Cover with plastic wrap; refrigerate 1 to 8 hours.

3. Vent plastic wrap. Microwave at MEDIUM (50% power) 20 minutes or until pasta is tender and hot. Sprinkle with cheese. Microwave at HIGH 3 minutes or just until cheese melts. Let stand, covered, 5 minutes before serving. *Makes 6 servings*

Ravioli with Homemade Tomato Sauce

Mediterranean Stew

1 medium butternut or acorn squash, peeled and cut into 1-inch cubes
2 cups unpeeled eggplant, cut into 1-inch cubes
2 cups sliced zucchini
1 can (15½ ounces) chickpeas (garbanzo beans), rinsed and drained
1 package (10 ounces) frozen cut okra
1 can (8 ounces) tomato sauce
1 cup chopped onion
1 medium tomato, chopped
1 medium carrot, thinly sliced
½ cup reduced-sodium vegetable broth
⅓ cup raisins
1 clove garlic, minced
½ teaspoon ground cumin
½ teaspoon ground turmeric
¼ to ½ teaspoon ground red pepper
¼ teaspoon ground cinnamon
¼ teaspoon paprika
6 to 8 cups hot cooked couscous or rice
Fresh parsley (optional)

Slow Cooker Directions

1. Combine squash, eggplant, zucchini, chickpeas, okra, tomato sauce, onion, tomato, carrot, broth, raisins, garlic, cumin, turmeric, red pepper, cinnamon and paprika in slow cooker; mix well.

2. Cover; cook on LOW 8 to 10 hours or until vegetables are crisp-tender.

3. Serve over couscous. Garnish with parsley, if desired.   *Makes 6 servings*

Mediterranean Stew

Broccoli & Cheddar Noodle Casserole

1 package (12 ounces) dry wide egg noodles
3 tablespoons margarine or butter, divided
2 cups chopped onions
4 cups broccoli flowerets
1 can (14.5 ounces) CONTADINA® Stewed Tomatoes, undrained
1 can (6 ounces) CONTADINA Tomato Paste
1 package (1½ ounces) spaghetti sauce seasoning mix
2 cups water
1 teaspoon garlic salt
1½ cups (6 ounces) shredded Cheddar cheese
½ cup CONTADINA Seasoned Italian Bread Crumbs

1. Cook noodles according to package directions; drain.

2. Meanwhile, melt 2 tablespoons margarine in 5-quart saucepan; sauté onions until tender.

3. Stir in broccoli, undrained tomatoes, tomato paste, seasoning mix, water and garlic salt. Bring to a boil. Reduce heat; simmer, uncovered, for 10 minutes, stirring occasionally. Stir in cooked noodles.

4. Layer half of the noodle mixture in 13×9×2-inch baking dish. Sprinkle with cheese. Layer with remaining noodle mixture.

5. Melt remaining 1 tablespoon margarine; stir in crumbs. Sprinkle over casserole; cover and bake in preheated 350°F oven 20 minutes. Uncover; bake 5 minutes.

Makes 6 servings

Prep Time: 25 minutes
Cook Time: 25 minutes

Broccoli & Cheddar Noodle Casserole

Farmstand Frittata

Nonstick cooking spray
½ cup chopped onion
1 medium red bell pepper, seeded and cut into thin strips
1 cup broccoli florets, blanched and drained
1 cup cooked, quartered unpeeled red potatoes
1 cup cholesterol-free egg substitute
6 egg whites
1 tablespoon chopped fresh parsley
½ teaspoon salt
¼ teaspoon black pepper
½ cup (2 ounces) shredded reduced-fat Cheddar cheese

1. Spray large nonstick ovenproof skillet with cooking spray; heat over medium heat until hot. Add onion and bell pepper; cook and stir 3 minutes or until crisp-tender.

2. Add broccoli and potatoes; cook and stir 1 to 2 minutes or until heated through.

3. Whisk together egg substitute, egg whites, parsley, salt and black pepper in medium bowl.

4. Spread vegetables into even layer in skillet. Pour egg white mixture over vegetables; cover and cook over medium heat 10 to 12 minutes or until egg mixture is set.

5. Meanwhile, preheat broiler. Top frittata with cheese. Broil 4 inches from heat 1 minute or until cheese is melted. Cut into four wedges.   *Makes 4 servings*

Cannellini Parmesan Casserole

2 tablespoons olive oil
1 cup chopped onion
2 teaspoons minced garlic
1 teaspoon dried oregano leaves
¼ teaspoon black pepper
2 cans (14½ ounces each) diced tomatoes with onion and garlic, undrained
1 jar (14 ounces) roasted red peppers, drained and cut into ½-inch pieces
2 cans (about 15 ounces each) white cannellini beans or Great Northern beans, rinsed and drained
1 teaspoon dried basil leaves *or* 1 tablespoon chopped fresh basil
¾ cup grated Parmesan cheese

1. Heat oil in Dutch oven over medium heat until hot. Add onion, garlic, oregano and black pepper; cook and stir 5 minutes or until onion is tender.

2. Increase heat to high. Add tomatoes with juice and red peppers; cover and bring to a boil.

3. Reduce heat to medium. Stir in beans; cover and simmer 5 minutes, stirring occasionally. Stir in basil and sprinkle with cheese.   *Makes 6 servings*

Prep and Cook Time: 20 minutes

Vegetarian Lasagna

    1 small eggplant, sliced into ½-inch rounds
½ teaspoon salt
    2 tablespoons olive oil, divided
    1 tablespoon butter
    8 ounces mushrooms, sliced
    1 small onion, diced
    1 can (26 ounces) pasta sauce
    1 teaspoon dried basil
    1 teaspoon dried oregano
    2 cups part-skim ricotta cheese
1½ cups (6 ounces) shredded Monterey Jack cheese
    1 cup grated Parmesan cheese, divided
    1 package (8 ounces) whole wheat lasagna noodles, cooked and
       drained
    1 medium zucchini, thinly sliced

Slow Cooker Directions

1. Sprinkle eggplant with salt; let sit 10 to 15 minutes. Rinse and pat dry; brush with 1 tablespoon olive oil. Brown on both sides in medium skillet over medium heat. Set aside.

2. Heat remaining 1 tablespoon olive oil and butter in same skillet over medium heat; cook and stir mushrooms and onion until softened. Stir in pasta sauce, basil and oregano. Set aside.

3. Combine ricotta cheese, Monterey Jack cheese and ½ cup Parmesan cheese in medium bowl. Set aside.

4. Spread ⅓ sauce mixture in bottom of slow cooker. Layer with ⅓ lasagna noodles, ½ eggplant, ½ cheese mixture. Repeat layers once. For last layer, use remaining ⅓ of lasagna noodles, zucchini, remaining ⅓ of sauce mixture and top with remaining ½ cup Parmesan.

5. Cover; cook on LOW 6 hours. Let sit 15 to 20 minutes before serving.

Makes 4 to 6 servings

Note: This recipe scored highly in our taste test; however, it is not a true slow cooker recipe as most of the ingredients are cooked separately before being added to the slow cooker.

Vegetarian Lasagna

Fire & Ice Brunch Skillet

1 (6.8-ounce) package RICE-A-RONI® Spanish Rice
2 tablespoons margarine or butter
1 (16-ounce) jar salsa
⅓ cup sour cream
¼ cup thinly sliced green onions
4 large eggs
1 cup (4 ounces) shredded Cheddar cheese
Chopped cilantro (optional)

1. In large skillet over medium heat, sauté rice-vermicelli mix with margarine until vermicelli is golden brown.

2. Slowly stir in 2 cups water, salsa and Special Seasonings; bring to a boil. Reduce heat to low. Cover; simmer 15 to 20 minutes or until rice is tender.

3. Stir in sour cream and green onions. Using large spoon, make 4 indentations in rice mixture. Break 1 egg into each indentation. Reduce heat to low. Cover; cook 8 minutes or until eggs are cooked to desired doneness.

4. Sprinkle cheese evenly over eggs and rice. Cover; let stand 3 minutes or until cheese is melted. Sprinkle with cilantro, if desired.   *Makes 4 servings*

Tip: A twist on Mexican-style huevos rancheros, serve this for brunch or as a light dinner.

Prep Time: 5 minutes
Cook Time: 30 minutes

Fire & Ice Brunch Skillet

Broccoli & Cheese Strata

2 cups chopped broccoli florets
4 slices firm white bread, ½-inch thick
4 teaspoons butter
1½ cups (6 ounces) shredded Cheddar cheese
1½ cups low-fat (1%) milk
3 eggs
½ teaspoon salt
½ teaspoon hot pepper sauce
⅛ teaspoon black pepper

Slow Cooker Directions

1. Cook broccoli in boiling water 10 minutes or until tender. Drain. Spread one side of each bread slice with 1 teaspoon butter. Arrange 2 slices bread, buttered sides up, in greased 1-quart casserole that will fit in slow cooker. Layer cheese, broccoli and remaining 2 bread slices, buttered sides down.

2. Beat milk, eggs, salt, pepper sauce and black pepper in medium bowl. Gradually pour over bread.

3. Place small wire rack in 5-quart slow cooker. Pour in 1 cup water. Place casserole on rack. Cover; cook on HIGH 3 hours.   *Makes 4 servings*

Broccoli & Cheese Strata

Baked Risotto with Asparagus, Spinach & Parmesan

1 tablespoon olive oil
1 cup finely chopped onion
1 cup arborio (risotto) rice
8 cups (8 to 10 ounces) spinach leaves, torn into pieces
2 cups chicken broth
¼ teaspoon salt
¼ teaspoon ground nutmeg
½ cup grated Parmesan cheese, divided
1½ cups diagonally sliced asparagus

1. Preheat oven to 400°F. Spray 13×9-inch baking dish with nonstick cooking spray.

2. Heat olive oil in large skillet over medium-high heat. Add onion; cook and stir 4 minutes or until tender. Add rice; stir to coat with oil.

3. Stir in spinach, a handful at a time, adding more as it wilts. Add broth, salt and nutmeg. Reduce heat and simmer 7 minutes. Stir in ¼ cup cheese.

4. Transfer to prepared baking dish. Cover tightly and bake 15 minutes.

5. Remove from oven and stir in asparagus; sprinkle with remaining ¼ cup cheese. Cover and bake 15 minutes more or until liquid is absorbed.   *Makes 6 servings*

Baked Risotto with Asparagus, Spinach & Parmesan

Hearty Manicotti

8 to 10 dry manicotti shells
1 package (10 ounces) frozen chopped spinach, thawed, squeezed dry
1 carton (15 ounces) ricotta cheese
1 egg, lightly beaten
½ cup (2 ounces) grated Parmesan cheese
⅛ teaspoon ground black pepper
2 cans (6 ounces each) CONTADINA® Italian Paste with Italian Seasonings
1⅓ cups water
½ cup (2 ounces) shredded mozzarella cheese

1. Cook pasta according to package directions; drain.

2. Meanwhile, combine spinach, ricotta cheese, egg, Parmesan cheese and pepper in medium bowl; mix well.

3. Spoon into manicotti shells. Place in ungreased 12×7½-inch baking dish.

4. Combine tomato paste and water in small bowl; pour over manicotti. Sprinkle with mozzarella cheese. Bake in preheated 350°F oven for 30 to 40 minutes or until heated through.   *Makes 4 to 5 servings*

Prep Time: 15 minutes
Cook Time: 40 minutes

Hearty Manicotti

Lasagna à la Zucchini

8 (2-inch-wide) uncooked lasagna noodles
3 medium zucchini, cut into thin slices
1 can (16 ounces) Italian-style sliced stewed tomatoes, drained
¼ pound sliced, fresh mushrooms
1 small onion, chopped
2 cloves garlic, minced
1 teaspoon dried Italian seasoning
¼ teaspoon salt
⅛ teaspoon black pepper
1 can (6 ounces) tomato paste
1 container (16 ounces) small curd cottage cheese
6 eggs, lightly beaten
¼ cup freshly grated Parmesan cheese
2 cups (8 ounces) shredded mozzarella cheese

1. Preheat oven to 350°F.

2. Cook lasagna noodles according to package directions until tender but still firm. Drain; set aside.

3. Combine zucchini, tomatoes, mushrooms, onion, garlic, Italian seasoning, salt and pepper in large skillet. Cook over medium-high heat 5 to 7 minutes or until zucchini is tender. Stir in tomato paste; remove from heat.

4. Combine cottage cheese, eggs and Parmesan cheese in medium bowl; stir until well blended.

5. Place 4 noodles on bottom of greased 13×9-inch baking dish. Pour ½ of egg mixture evenly over noodles. Cover egg mixture with ½ of tomato mixture; sprinkle with 1½ cups mozzarella. Repeat layers with remaining ingredients, ending with ½ cup mozzarella.

6. Bake covered 30 minutes. Uncover; bake 10 minutes or until heated through. Let stand 10 minutes before serving.   *Makes 8 to 10 servings*

Spinach and Mushroom Enchiladas

2 packages (10 ounces each) frozen chopped spinach, thawed
1½ cups sliced mushrooms
1 can (15 ounces) pinto beans, drained and rinsed
3 teaspoons chili powder, divided
¼ teaspoon red pepper flakes
1 can (8 ounces) reduced-sodium tomato sauce
2 tablespoons water
½ teaspoon hot pepper sauce
8 (8-inch) corn tortillas
1 cup (4 ounces) shredded Monterey Jack cheese
Shredded lettuce (optional)
Chopped tomatoes (optional)
Reduced-fat sour cream (optional)

1. Combine spinach, mushrooms, beans, 2 teaspoons chili powder and red pepper flakes in large skillet over medium heat. Cook and stir 5 minutes; remove from heat.

2. Combine tomato sauce, water, remaining 1 teaspoon chili powder and pepper sauce in medium skillet. Dip tortillas into tomato sauce mixture; stack tortillas on waxed paper.

3. Divide spinach filling into 8 portions. Spoon onto center of tortillas; roll up and place in 11×8-inch microwavable dish. (Secure rolls with toothpicks, if desired.) Spread remaining tomato sauce mixture over enchiladas. Cover with vented plastic wrap.

4. Microwave, uncovered, at MEDIUM (50%) 10 minutes or until heated through. Sprinkle with cheese. Microwave at MEDIUM 3 minutes or until cheese is melted. Serve with lettuce, tomatoes and sour cream, if desired.   *Makes 4 servings*

Roasted Vegetables with Fettuccine

2 pounds assorted fresh vegetables*
1 envelope LIPTON® RECIPE SECRETS® Savory Herb with Garlic Soup
   Mix**
3 tablespoons BERTOLLI® Olive Oil
½ cup light cream, whipping or heavy cream or half-and-half
¼ cup grated Parmesan cheese
8 ounces fettuccine or linguine, cooked and drained

*Use any combination of the following, cut into 1-inch chunks: zucchini, yellow squash, red, green or yellow bell peppers, carrots, celery, onion and mushrooms.

**Also terrific with LIPTON® Recipe Secrets® Golden Onion Soup Mix.

Preheat oven to 450°F. In 13×9-inch baking or roasting pan, combine vegetables, soup mix and oil until evenly coated.

Bake uncovered, stirring once, 20 minutes or until vegetables are tender. Stir in light cream and cheese until evenly coated.

Toss with hot fettuccine. Serve, if desired, with additional grated Parmesan cheese and freshly ground black pepper.

Makes about 2 main-dish or 4 side-dish servings

Roasted Vegetables with Fettuccine

Cheesy Baked Barley

2 cups water
½ cup medium pearled barley
½ teaspoon salt, divided
   Nonstick cooking spray
½ cup diced onion
½ cup diced zucchini
½ cup diced red bell pepper
1 ½ teaspoons all-purpose flour
   Seasoned pepper
¾ cup fat-free (skim) milk
   1 cup (4 ounces) shredded reduced-fat Italian cheese blend, divided
   1 tablespoon Dijon mustard

1. Bring water to a boil in 1-quart saucepan. Add barley and ¼ teaspoon salt. Cover; reduce heat and simmer 45 minutes or until barley is tender and most of the water has evaporated. Let stand covered, 5 minutes.

2. Preheat oven to 375°F. Spray medium skillet with cooking spray. Cook onion, zucchini and bell pepper over medium-low heat about 10 minutes or until soft. Stir in flour, remaining ¼ teaspoon salt and seasoned pepper to taste; cook 1 to 2 minutes. Add milk, stirring constantly; cook and stir until slightly thickened. Remove from heat and add barley, ¾ cup cheese and mustard; stir until cheese is melted.

3. Spread in even layer in casserole. Sprinkle with remaining ¼ cup cheese. Bake 20 minutes or until hot. Preheat broiler. Broil casserole 1 to 2 minutes or until cheese is lightly browned. *Makes 2 servings*

Cheesy Baked Barley

Layered Mexican Tortilla Cheese Casserole

1 can (14½ ounces) salsa-style or Mexican-style stewed tomatoes, undrained
½ cup chopped fresh cilantro, divided
2 tablespoons fresh lime juice
Nonstick vegetable cooking spray
6 (6-inch) corn tortillas, torn into 1½-inch pieces
1 can (15 ounces) black beans, rinsed and drained
1 can (8 ounces) whole kernel corn, drained *or* 1 cup frozen whole kernel corn, thawed
2 cups (8 ounces) SARGENTO® Mexican Blend Shredded Cheese

1. In small bowl, combine tomatoes, ¼ cup cilantro and lime juice; set aside.

2. Coat 8-inch square baking dish with cooking spray. Arrange ¼ of tortillas in bottom of dish; spoon ¼ of tomato mixture over tortillas. Top with ¼ of beans, ¼ of corn and ¼ of cheese. Repeat layering 3 more times with remaining tortillas, tomato mixture, beans, corn and cheese.

3. Bake uncovered at 375°F 25 minutes or until cheese is melted and sauce is bubbly. Sprinkle with remaining ¼ cup cilantro. Let stand 10 minutes before serving.
Makes 4 servings

Layered Mexican Tortilla Cheese Casserole

Vegetarian Paella

    1 tablespoon olive oil
    1 medium onion, chopped
    1 serrano pepper,* finely chopped
    1 red bell pepper, diced
    1 green bell pepper, diced
    3 cloves garlic, minced
    ½ teaspoon saffron threads, crushed
    ½ teaspoon paprika
    1 cup uncooked long-grain white rice
    3 cups water
    1 can (15 ounces) chick-peas (garbanzo beans), rinsed and drained
    1 can (14 ounces) artichoke hearts in water, drained and cut into
        halves
    1 cup frozen green peas
    1½ teaspoons grated lemon peel
        Fresh bay leaves (optional)
        Lemon slices (optional)

*Serrano peppers can sting and irritate the skin; wear rubber gloves when handling peppers and do not touch eyes. Wash hands after handling.

1. Preheat oven to 375°F. Heat oil in heavy ovenproof skillet over medium-high heat. Add onion, serrano pepper and bell peppers; cook and stir about 7 minutes.

2. Add garlic, saffron and paprika; cook 3 minutes. Add rice; cook and stir 1 minute. Add water, chick-peas, artichoke hearts, green peas and lemon peel; mix well.

3. Cover; bake 25 minutes or until rice is tender. Garnish with fresh bay leaves and lemon slices, if desired. *Makes 6 servings*

Quick Veg•All® Enchiladas

1 can (15 ounces) VEG•ALL® Original Mixed Vegetables, drained
1 can (15 ounces) refried beans
8 (6-inch) corn tortillas
1 can (10 ounces) enchilada sauce
1 cup shredded cheddar cheese
1 cup sour cream
½ cup chopped green onions
½ cup chopped ripe olives

Preheat oven to 350°F. Combine Veg•All and beans in medium bowl. Divide mixture and place in center of each tortilla; roll up. Place rolled tortillas in baking dish. Cover tortillas with enchilada sauce and cheese. Bake for 30 minutes. Top with sour cream, green onions, and ripe olives. *Makes 4 servings*

Note: If tortillas unfold as you are assembling them, turn seam-side down.

Prep Time: 7 minutes
Cook Time: 30 minutes

Skillet Pesto Tortellini

1¼ cups water
1¼ cups milk
1 envelope (1.2 ounces) creamy pesto sauce mix
1 package (16 ounces) frozen vegetable medley
1 package (12 ounces) frozen tortellini
Dash ground red pepper
½ cup (2 ounces) shredded mozzarella cheese

1. Blend water, milk and sauce mix in large deep skillet. Bring to a boil over high heat. Stir in vegetables, tortellini and ground red pepper; return to a boil.

2. Cook vegetables and tortellini, uncovered, over medium-high heat 8 to 10 minutes or until tortellini is tender and sauce has thickened, stirring occasionally.

3. Sprinkle with cheese just before serving. *Makes 4 servings*

Prep and Cook Time: 22 minutes

Mushroom & Onion Egg Bake

1 tablespoon vegetable oil
4 green onions, chopped
4 ounces sliced mushrooms
1 cup low-fat (1%) cottage cheese
1 cup sour cream
6 eggs
2 tablespoons all-purpose flour
¼ teaspoon salt
⅛ teaspoon black pepper
  Dash hot pepper sauce

1. Preheat oven to 350°F. Grease shallow 1-quart baking dish.

2. Heat oil in medium skillet over medium heat. Add onions and mushrooms; cook until tender. Set aside.

3. In blender or food processor, process cottage cheese until almost smooth. Add sour cream, eggs, flour, salt, black pepper and hot pepper sauce; process until combined. Stir in onions and mushrooms. Pour into prepared baking dish. Bake about 40 minutes or until knife inserted near center comes out clean.

Makes about 6 servings

Mushroom & Onion Egg Bake

Stuffed Bell Peppers

1 package (8½ ounces) cornbread mix *plus* ingredients to prepare
6 green bell peppers
1 large onion, thinly sliced
1 teaspoon olive oil
1 can (16 ounces) no-salt-added diced tomatoes, drained
1 package (10 ounces) frozen corn, thawed and drained
1 can (2¼ ounces) sliced black olives, drained
⅓ cup raisins
1 tablespoon chili powder
1 teaspoon ground sage
1 cup (4 ounces) shredded reduced-fat Monterey Jack cheese,
divided
Cherry tomato halves and fresh herbs for garnish (optional)

Prepare cornbread according to package directions. Cut into cubes. *Reduce oven temperature to 350°F.* Slice tops off bell peppers; discard stems and seeds. Finely chop tops to equal 1 cup; set aside. Rinse peppers. Bring 2 to 3 inches water to a boil over high heat in large saucepan. Add 1 or more peppers and boil 1 minute, turning peppers with tongs to blanch evenly. Rinse with cold water; drain. Repeat with remaining peppers.

Place onion and oil in Dutch oven. Cover and cook over medium-high heat, stirring occasionally, 8 to 10 minutes or until onion is tender and browned. Add 1 to 2 tablespoons water, if needed, to prevent sticking. Add chopped bell pepper; stir 1 minute more. Remove from heat. Add tomatoes, corn, olives, raisins, chili powder and sage; stir. Stir in corn bread (it will crumble) and ¾ cup cheese. Spoon filling into peppers. Top with remaining ¼ cup cheese. Place peppers in baking dish; bake 20 to 30 minutes or until heated through. Garnish, if desired.   *Makes 6 servings*

Stuffed Bell Peppers

Pesto Lasagna

1 package (16 ounces) uncooked lasagna noodles
3 tablespoons olive oil
1½ cups chopped onion
3 cloves garlic, finely chopped
3 packages (10 ounces each) frozen chopped spinach, thawed and
    squeezed dry
Salt
Black pepper
3 cups (24 ounces) ricotta cheese
1½ cups prepared pesto sauce
¾ cup (3 ounces) grated Parmesan cheese
½ cup pine nuts, toasted
6 cups (16 ounces) shredded mozzarella cheese
Strips of roasted red pepper (optional)

1. Preheat oven to 350°F. Oil 13×9-inch casserole or lasagna pan. Partially cook lasagna noodles according to package directions.

2. Heat oil in large skillet. Cook and stir onion and garlic until transparent. Add spinach; cook and stir about 5 minutes. Season with salt and pepper. Transfer to large bowl.

3. Add ricotta cheese, pesto, Parmesan cheese and pine nuts to spinach mixture; mix well.

4. Layer 5 lasagna noodles, slightly overlapping, in prepared casserole. Top with ⅓ of spinach-ricotta mixture and ⅓ of mozzarella. Repeat layers twice.

5. Bake about 35 minutes or until hot and bubbly. Garnish with red pepper, if desired.   *Makes 8 servings*

Pesto Lasagna

Moroccan Supper

1 (7.2-ounce) package RICE-A-RONI® Rice Pilaf
½ cup chopped onion
2 cloves garlic, minced
2 tablespoons margarine or olive oil
1 teaspoon ground cumin
¼ teaspoon ground cinnamon
1 (15-ounce) can garbanzo beans or chick peas, rinsed and drained
1½ cups broccoli flowerets
¼ cup dried apricots, slivered or raisins
⅓ cup slivered or sliced almonds, toasted
¼ cup chopped cilantro (optional)

1. In large skillet over medium heat, sauté rice-pasta mix, onion and garlic with margarine until pasta is light golden brown.

2. Slowly stir in 2 cups water, cumin, cinnamon and Special Seasonings; bring to a boil. Cover; reduce heat to low. Simmer 10 minutes.

3. Stir in beans, broccoli and apricots. Cover; simmer 10 to 12 minutes or until rice is tender. Serve topped with almonds and cilantro, if desired.   *Makes 4 servings*

Tip: For a Southwestern flair, use black beans, 1½ cups corn and ¼ teaspoon chili powder instead of garbanzo beans, apricots and cinnamon.

Prep Time: 10 minutes
Cook Time: 30 minutes

Moroccan Supper

Vegetable & Tofu Gratin

Nonstick cooking spray
1 teaspoon olive oil
¾ cup thinly sliced fennel bulb
¾ cup thinly sliced onion
2 cloves garlic, minced
¾ cup cooked brown rice
2 tablespoons balsamic or red wine vinegar, divided
2 teaspoons dried Italian seasoning, divided
3 ounces firm tofu, crumbled
¼ cup crumbled feta cheese
2 to 3 ripe plum tomatoes, sliced ¼ inch thick
1 medium zucchini, sliced ¼ inch thick
⅛ teaspoon salt
⅛ teaspoon black pepper
¼ cup fresh bread crumbs
2 tablespoons freshly grated Parmesan cheese

1. Preheat oven to 400°F. Spray 1-quart shallow baking dish with nonstick cooking spray.

2. Spray medium skillet with cooking spray. Heat oil in medium skillet over medium heat until hot. Add fennel and onion. Cook about 10 minutes or until tender and lightly browned, stirring frequently. Add garlic; cook and stir 1 minute. Spread over bottom of prepared baking dish.

3. Combine rice, 1 tablespoon vinegar and ½ teaspoon Italian seasoning in small bowl. Spread over onion mixture.

4. Combine tofu, feta cheese, remaining 1 tablespoon vinegar and 1 teaspoon Italian seasoning in same small bowl; toss to combine. Spoon over rice.

5. Top with alternating rows of tomato and zucchini slices. Sprinkle with salt and pepper.

6. Combine bread crumbs, Parmesan cheese and remaining ½ teaspoon Italian seasoning in small bowl. Sprinkle over top. Spray bread crumb topping lightly with nonstick cooking spray. Bake 30 minutes or until heated through and topping is browned. *Makes 2 servings*

Vegetable & Tofu Gratin

Indian Vegetable Curry

2 to 3 teaspoons curry powder
1 can (16 ounces) sliced potatoes, drained
1 bag (16 ounces) BIRDS EYE® frozen Farm Fresh Mixtures Broccoli,
**   Cauliflower and Carrots**
1 can (15 ounces) chick-peas, drained
1 can (14½ ounces) stewed tomatoes
1 can (13¾ ounces) vegetable or chicken broth
2 tablespoons cornstarch

● Stir curry powder in large skillet over high heat until fragrant, about 30 seconds.

● Stir in potatoes, vegetables, chick-peas and tomatoes; bring to a boil. Reduce heat to medium-high; cover and cook 8 minutes.

● Blend broth with cornstarch; stir into vegetables. Cook until thickened.

Makes about 6 servings

Serving Suggestion: Add cooked chicken for a heartier main dish. Serve with white or brown rice.

Prep Time: 5 minutes
Cook Time: 15 minutes

Three-Cheese Penne

2 cups uncooked penne pasta
Nonstick cooking spray
2 slices whole wheat bread, cut into cubes
2 cups fat-free cottage cheese
2 cups (8 ounces) shredded reduced-fat Cheddar cheese
1 cup chopped Roma tomatoes, divided
⅓ cup sliced green onions
¼ cup grated Parmesan cheese
¼ cup reduced-fat (2%) milk

1. Cook pasta according to package directions, omitting salt. Drain and rinse well under cold water until pasta is cool; drain well.

2. Spray large nonstick skillet with cooking spray; heat over medium heat until hot. Place bread cubes in skillet; spray bread cubes lightly with cooking spray. Cook and stir 5 minutes or until bread cubes are browned and crisp.

3. Preheat oven to 350°F. Combine pasta, cottage cheese, Cheddar cheese, ¾ cup tomatoes, green onions, Parmesan cheese and milk in medium bowl. Spray 2-quart casserole with nonstick cooking spray. Place pasta mixture in casserole. Top with remaining ¼ cup tomatoes and cooled bread cubes.

4. Bake 20 minutes or until heated through. Garnish, if desired.

Makes 6 servings

Eggplant Squash Bake

½ cup chopped onion
1 clove garlic, minced
  Nonstick olive oil cooking spray
1 cup part-skim ricotta cheese
1 jar (4 ounces) diced pimientos, drained
¼ cup grated Parmesan cheese
2 tablespoons fat-free (skim) milk
1½ teaspoons dried marjoram
¾ teaspoon dried tarragon
¼ teaspoon salt
¼ teaspoon ground nutmeg
¼ teaspoon black pepper
1 cup no-sugar-added meatless spaghetti sauce, divided
½ pound eggplant, peeled and cut into thin crosswise slices
2 medium (6 ounces) zucchini, cut in half then lengthwise into thin slices
2 medium (6 ounces) yellow summer squash, cut in half then lengthwise into thin slices
2 tablespoons shredded part-skim mozzarella cheese

Microwave Directions

1. Combine onion and garlic in medium microwavable bowl. Spray lightly with cooking spray. Microwave at HIGH 1 minute.

2. Add ricotta, pimientos, Parmesan, milk, marjoram, tarragon, salt, nutmeg and pepper. Spray 9- or 10-inch round microwavable baking dish with cooking spray. Spread ⅓ cup spaghetti sauce in bottom of dish.

3. Layer half of eggplant, zucchini and summer squash in dish; top with ricotta mixture. Layer remaining eggplant, zucchini and summer squash over ricotta mixture. Top with remaining ⅔ cup spaghetti sauce.

4. Cover with vented plastic wrap. Microwave at HIGH 17 to 19 minutes or until vegetables are tender, rotating dish every 6 minutes. Top with mozzarella cheese. Let stand 10 minutes before serving.   *Makes 4 servings*

Eggplant Squash Bake

Cheddar and Leek Strata

8 eggs, lightly beaten
2 cups milk
½ cup ale or beer
2 cloves garlic, minced
¼ teaspoon salt
¼ teaspoon black pepper
1 loaf (16 ounces) sourdough bread, cut into ½-inch cubes
2 small leeks, coarsely chopped
1 red bell pepper, chopped
1½ cups (6 ounces) shredded Swiss cheese
1½ cups (6 ounces) shredded sharp Cheddar cheese
Fresh sage sprigs for garnish

1. Combine eggs, milk, ale, garlic, salt and black pepper in large bowl. Beat until well blended.

2. Place ½ of bread cubes on bottom of greased 13×9-inch baking dish. Sprinkle ½ of leeks and ½ of bell pepper over bread cubes. Top with ¾ cup Swiss cheese and ¾ cup Cheddar cheese. Repeat layers with remaining ingredients, ending with Cheddar cheese.

3. Pour egg mixture evenly over top. Cover tightly with plastic wrap or foil. Weigh top of strata down with slightly smaller baking dish. Refrigerate strata at least 2 hours or overnight.

4. Preheat oven to 350°F. Bake, uncovered, 40 to 45 minutes or until center is set. Garnish with fresh sage, if desired. Serve immediately. *Makes 12 servings*

Cheddar and Leek Strata

Vegetarian Sausage Rice

2 cups chopped green bell peppers
1 can (15½ ounces) dark kidney beans, drained and rinsed
**1 can (14½ ounces) diced tomatoes with green bell peppers and
    onions, undrained**
1 cup chopped onion
1 cup sliced celery
1 cup water, divided
¾ cup uncooked long-grain white rice
1¼ teaspoons salt
1 teaspoon hot pepper sauce
½ teaspoon dried thyme leaves
½ teaspoon red pepper flakes
3 bay leaves
1 package (8 ounces) vegetable protein breakfast patties, thawed
2 tablespoons extra virgin olive oil
½ cup chopped fresh parsley
**   Additional hot pepper sauce (optional)**

Slow Cooker Directions

1. Combine bell peppers, beans, tomatoes with juice, onion, celery, ½ cup water, rice, salt, pepper sauce, thyme, pepper flakes and bay leaves in slow cooker. Cover; cook on LOW 4 to 5 hours. Remove and discard bay leaves.

2. Dice breakfast patties. Heat oil in large nonstick skillet over medium-high heat. Add patties; cook 2 minutes or until lightly browned, scraping bottom of skillet occasionally.

3. Place patties in slow cooker. *Do not stir.* Add remaining ½ cup water to skillet; bring to a boil over high heat 1 minute, scraping up bits on bottom of skillet. Add liquid and parsley to slow cooker; stir gently to blend. Serve immediately with additional hot pepper sauce, if desired. *Makes 8 cups*

Vegetarian Sausage Rice

Zucornchile Rajas Bake

2 cups tomato sauce
2 tablespoons chili powder
2 tablespoons tomato paste
1 tablespoon cider vinegar
1 teaspoon ground cumin
½ teaspoon salt
½ teaspoon garlic powder
¼ teaspoon ground red pepper
6 corn tortillas
  Vegetable oil for frying
1 pound zucchini, thinly sliced (about 3 cups)
1½ cups (6 ounces) shredded Monterey Jack or manchego cheese,*
  divided
1 cup corn kernels
1 can (4 ounces) diced green chilies, drained
½ to 1 cup sour cream
3 green onions, chopped

*Manchego cheese is a popular Spanish cheese that melts easily. Look for it at specialty food markets.

1. Preheat oven to 350°F. Oil 13×9-inch baking dish.

2. Combine tomato sauce, chili powder, tomato paste, vinegar, cumin, salt, garlic powder and red pepper in medium saucepan. Bring to a boil over high heat; reduce heat to low and simmer 10 minutes, stirring occasionally.

3. Meanwhile, cut tortillas into ¼-inch-wide strips. Heat enough oil to cover bottom of medium skillet by ½ inch. Fry tortilla strips in batches until crisp; drain on paper towels.

4. Steam zucchini 5 minutes; drain. Transfer to large bowl. Add ¾ cup cheese, corn, chilies and tortilla strips. Toss lightly to combine; spoon into prepared baking dish. Spread tomato sauce mixture over zucchini mixture and top with remaining ¾ cup cheese. Bake 30 minutes or until heated through.

5. Spread sour cream over top and sprinkle with green onions. Serve immediately.

Makes 6 to 8 servings

Zucornchile Rajas Bake

Vegetable Medley Quiche

   Nonstick cooking spray
2 cups frozen diced potatoes with onions and peppers, thawed
**1 (16-ounce) package frozen mixed vegetables (such as zucchini,
   carrots and beans), thawed and drained**
**1 can (10¾ ounces) reduced-fat condensed cream of mushroom
   soup, divided**
1 cup cholesterol-free egg substitute *or* 4 eggs
½ cup grated Parmesan cheese, divided
¼ cup fat-free (skim) milk
¼ teaspoon dried dill weed
¼ teaspoon dried thyme leaves
¼ teaspoon dried oregano leaves
   Dash salt and black pepper (optional)

1. Preheat oven to 400°F. Spray 9-inch pie plate with cooking spray; press potatoes onto bottom and side of pan to form crust. Spray potatoes lightly with cooking spray. Bake 15 minutes.

2. Combine mixed vegetables, half of soup, egg substitute and ¼ cup cheese in small bowl; mix well. Pour egg mixture into potato shell; sprinkle with remaining ¼ cup cheese. *Reduce oven temperature to 375°F.* Bake 35 to 40 minutes or until set. Cut quiche into 6 wedges before serving.

3. Combine remaining soup, milk and seasonings in small saucepan; mix well. Simmer over low heat 5 minutes or until heated through. Serve sauce with quiche wedges. *Makes 6 servings*

Vegetable Medley Quiche

From the Sea

Tempting Tuna Parmesano

1 package (9 ounces) refrigerated fresh angel hair pasta
¼ cup butter or margarine
2 large cloves garlic, minced
1 cup whipping cream
1 cup frozen peas
¼ teaspoon salt
1 can (6 ounces) white tuna in water, drained
¼ cup grated Parmesan cheese, plus additional for serving
    Black pepper

1. Fill large deep skillet ¾ full with water. Cover and bring to a boil over high heat.

2. Add pasta to skillet; boil 1 to 2 minutes or until pasta is al dente. Do not overcook. Drain; set aside.

3. Add butter and garlic to skillet; cook over medium-high heat until butter is melted and sizzling. Stir in cream, peas and salt; bring to a boil.

4. Break tuna into chunks and stir into skillet with ¼ cup cheese. Return pasta to skillet. Cook until heated through; toss gently. Serve with additional cheese and pepper to taste. *Makes 2 to 3 servings*

Serving Suggestion: Serve with a tossed romaine and tomato salad with Italian dressing.

Prep and Cook Time: 16 minutes

Tempting Tuna Parmesano

Lemon Shrimp

1 package (12 ounces) uncooked egg noodles
½ cup (1 stick) butter, softened
2 pounds cooked shrimp
3 tomatoes, chopped
1 cup shredded carrots
1 cup chicken broth
1 can (4 ounces) sliced mushrooms, drained
2 tablespoons fresh lemon juice
2 cloves garlic, chopped
½ teaspoon celery seed
¼ teaspoon black pepper

1. Preheat oven to 350°F.

2. Cook noodles according to package directions. Drain and mix with butter in large bowl, stirring until butter is melted and noodles are evenly coated. Add remaining ingredients and mix again. Transfer to 3-quart casserole.

3. Bake 15 to 20 minutes or until heated through.   *Makes 8 servings*

Lemon Shrimp

Elegant Crabmeat Frittata

3 tablespoons butter or margarine, divided
¼ pound fresh mushrooms, sliced
2 green onions, cut into thin slices
8 eggs, separated
¼ cup milk
¼ teaspoon salt
½ teaspoon hot pepper sauce
½ pound lump crabmeat or imitation crabmeat, flaked and picked
  over to remove any shells
½ cup (2 ounces) shredded Swiss cheese

1. Melt 2 tablespoons butter in large ovenproof skillet over medium-high heat. Add mushrooms and onions; cook and stir 3 to 5 minutes or until vegetables are tender. Remove from skillet; set aside.

2. Beat egg yolks with electric mixer at high speed until slightly thickened and lemon color. Stir in milk, salt and hot pepper sauce.

3. Beat egg whites in clean large bowl with electric mixer at high speed until foamy. Gradually add to egg yolk mixture, whisking just until blended.

4. Melt remaining 1 tablespoon butter in skillet. Pour egg mixture into skillet. Cook until egg is almost set. Remove from heat.

5. Preheat broiler. Broil frittata 4 to 6 inches from heat until top is set. Top with crabmeat, mushroom mixture and cheese. Return frittata to broiler; broil until cheese is melted. Garnish, if desired. Serve immediately.   *Makes 4 servings*

Elegant Crabmeat Frittata

Flounder Fillets over Zesty Lemon Rice

¼ cup butter
3 tablespoons fresh lemon juice
2 teaspoons chicken bouillon granules
½ teaspoon black pepper
1 cup cooked rice
1 package (10 ounces) frozen chopped broccoli, thawed
1 cup (4 ounces) shredded sharp Cheddar cheese
1 pound flounder fillets
½ teaspoon paprika

1. Preheat oven to 375°F. Spray 2-quart casserole with nonstick cooking spray.

2. Melt butter in small saucepan over medium heat. Add lemon juice, bouillon granules and pepper; cook and stir 2 minutes or until bouillon granules dissolve.

3. Combine rice, broccoli, cheese and ¼ cup lemon sauce in medium bowl; spread on bottom of prepared dish. Place fillets over rice mixture. Pour remaining lemon sauce over fillets.

4. Bake, uncovered, 20 minutes or until fish flakes easily when tested with fork. Sprinkle evenly with paprika. *Makes 6 servings*

Flounder Fillets over Zesty Lemon Rice

Spicy Tuna and Linguine with Garlic and Pine Nuts

2 tablespoons olive oil
4 cloves garlic, minced
2 cups sliced mushrooms
½ cup chopped onion
½ teaspoon crushed red pepper
2½ cups chopped plum tomatoes
1 can (14½ ounces) chicken broth plus water to equal 2 cups
½ teaspoon salt
¼ teaspoon coarsely ground black pepper
1 package (9 ounces) uncooked fresh linguine
1 (7-ounce) pouch of STARKIST Flavor Fresh Pouch® Albacore Tuna
⅓ cup chopped fresh cilantro
⅓ cup toasted pine nuts or almonds

In 12-inch skillet, heat olive oil over medium-high heat; sauté garlic, mushrooms, onion and red pepper until golden brown. Add tomatoes, chicken broth mixture, salt and black pepper; bring to a boil.

Separate uncooked linguine into strands; place in skillet and spoon sauce over. Reduce heat to simmer; cook, covered, 4 more minutes or until cooked through. Toss gently; add tuna and cilantro and toss again. Sprinkle with pine nuts.

Makes 4 to 6 servings

Spicy Tuna and Linguine with Garlic and Pine Nuts

Pasta with Salmon and Dill

6 ounces uncooked mafalda pasta
1 tablespoon olive oil
2 ribs celery, sliced
1 small red onion, chopped
1 can (10¾ ounces) condensed cream of celery soup, undiluted
¼ cup reduced-fat mayonnaise
¼ cup dry white wine
3 tablespoons chopped fresh parsley
1 teaspoon dried dill weed
1 can (7½ ounces) pink salmon, drained
½ cup dry bread crumbs
1 tablespoon butter, melted
Fresh dill sprigs (optional)

1. Preheat oven to 350°F. Spray 1-quart square baking dish with nonstick cooking spray.

2. Cook pasta according to package directions until al dente; drain and set aside.

3. Meanwhile, heat oil in medium skillet over medium-high heat until hot. Add celery and onion; cook and stir 2 minutes or until vegetables are tender. Set aside.

4. Combine soup, mayonnaise, wine, parsley and dill weed in large bowl. Stir in pasta, vegetables and salmon until pasta is well coated. Pour salmon mixture into prepared dish.

5. Combine bread crumbs and butter in small bowl; sprinkle evenly over casserole. Bake, uncovered, 25 minutes or until hot and bubbly. Garnish with dill sprigs, if desired.
Makes 4 servings

Pasta with Salmon and Dill

Herb-Baked Fish & Rice

1½ cups hot chicken bouillon
½ cup uncooked regular rice
¼ teaspoon Italian seasoning
¼ teaspoon garlic powder
1 package (10 ounces) frozen chopped broccoli, thawed and
    drained
1⅓ cups *French's*® French Fried Onions, divided
1 tablespoon grated Parmesan cheese
1 pound unbreaded fish fillets, thawed if frozen
    Paprika (optional)
½ cup (2 ounces) shredded Cheddar cheese

Preheat oven to 375°F. In 12×8-inch baking dish, combine hot bouillon, uncooked rice and seasonings. Bake, covered, at 375°F for 10 minutes. Top with broccoli, ⅔ cup French Fried Onions and the Parmesan cheese. Place fish fillets diagonally down center of dish; sprinkle fish lightly with paprika. Bake, covered, at 375°F for 20 to 25 minutes or until fish flakes easily with fork. Stir rice. Top fish with Cheddar cheese and remaining ⅔ cup French Fried Onions; bake, uncovered, 3 minutes or until onions are golden brown.   *Makes 3 to 4 servings*

Microwave Directions: In 12×8-inch microwave-safe dish, prepare rice mixture as above, except reduce bouillon to 1¼ cups. Cook, covered, on HIGH 5 minutes, stirring halfway through cooking time. Stir in broccoli, ⅔ cup onions and the Parmesan cheese. Arrange fish fillets in single layer on top of rice mixture; sprinkle fish lightly with paprika. Cook, covered, on MEDIUM (50-60%) 18 to 20 minutes or until fish flakes easily with fork and rice is done. Rotate dish halfway through cooking time. Top fish with Cheddar cheese and remaining ⅔ cup onions; cook, uncovered, on HIGH 1 minute or until cheese melts. Let stand 5 minutes.

Herb-Baked Fish & Rice

Veggie Mac and Tuna

1½ cups (6 ounces) elbow macaroni
3 tablespoons butter or margarine
1 small onion, chopped
½ medium red bell pepper, chopped
½ medium green bell pepper, chopped
¼ cup all-purpose flour
1¾ cups milk
8 ounces cubed light pasteurized process cheese product
½ teaspoon dried marjoram leaves
1 package (10 ounces) frozen peas
1 can (9 ounces) tuna in water, drained

Slow Cooker Directions

1. Cook macaroni according to package directions until just tender; drain.

2. Melt butter in medium saucepan over medium heat. Add onion and bell peppers. Cook and stir 5 minutes or until tender. Add flour. Stir constantly over medium heat 2 minutes. Stir in milk and bring to a boil. Boil, stirring constantly, until thickened. Reduce heat to low; add cheese and marjoram. Stir until cheese is melted.

3. Combine macaroni, cheese sauce, peas and tuna in slow cooker. Cover; cook on LOW 2½ hours or until bubbly at edge. *Makes 6 servings*

Veggie Mac and Tuna

Jambalaya

1 teaspoon vegetable oil
½ pound 99% fat-free smoked deli ham, cubed
½ pound smoked sausage, cut into ¼-inch-thick slices
1 large onion, chopped
1 large green bell pepper, chopped (about 1½ cups)
3 ribs celery, chopped (about 1 cup)
3 cloves garlic, minced
1 can (28 ounces) diced tomatoes, undrained
1 can (10½ ounces) fat-free reduced-sodium chicken broth
1 cup uncooked rice
1 tablespoon Worcestershire sauce
1 teaspoon salt
1 teaspoon dried thyme leaves
½ teaspoon black pepper
¼ teaspoon ground red pepper
1 package (12 ounces) frozen ready-to-cook shrimp, thawed
Fresh chives (optional)

1. Preheat oven to 350°F. Spray 13×9-inch baking dish with nonstick cooking spray.

2. Heat oil in large skillet over medium-high heat until hot. Add ham and sausage. Cook and stir 5 minutes or until sausage is lightly browned on both sides. Remove from skillet and place in prepared dish. Place onion, bell pepper, celery and garlic in same skillet; cook and stir 3 minutes. Add to sausage mixture.

3. Combine tomatoes with juice, broth, rice, Worcestershire, salt, thyme, black and red peppers in same skillet; bring to a boil over high heat. Reduce heat to low and simmer 3 minutes. Pour over sausage mixture and stir until combined.

4. Cover tightly with foil and bake 45 minutes or until rice is almost tender. Remove from oven; place shrimp on top of rice mixture. Bake, uncovered, 10 minutes or until shrimp are pink and opaque. Garnish with chives, if desired.   *Makes 8 servings*

Jambalaya

Fish Broccoli Casserole

1 package (10 ounces) frozen broccoli spears, thawed, drained
1 cup cooked flaked Florida whitefish
1 can (10¾ ounces) condensed cream of mushroom soup
½ cup milk
¼ teaspoon salt
⅛ teaspoon freshly ground black pepper
½ cup crushed potato chips

Preheat oven to 425°F. Grease 1½-quart casserole. Layer broccoli in prepared casserole. Combine fish, soup, milk, salt and pepper in large bowl.

Spread fish mixture over broccoli. Sprinkle with potato chips. Bake 12 to 15 minutes or until golden brown. *Makes 4 servings*

Favorite recipe from **Florida Department of Agriculture and Consumer Services, Bureau of Seafood and Aquaculture**

Seafood Newburg Casserole

1 can (10¾ ounces) condensed cream of shrimp soup, undiluted
½ cup half-and-half
1 tablespoon dry sherry
¼ teaspoon ground red pepper
3 cups cooked rice
2 cans (6 ounces each) lump crabmeat, drained
¼ pound raw medium shrimp, peeled and deveined
¼ pound raw bay scallops
1 jar (4 ounces) pimientos, drained and chopped
¼ cup finely chopped fresh parsley

1. Preheat oven to 350°F. Spray 2½-quart casserole with nonstick cooking spray.

2. Whisk together soup, half-and-half, sherry and red pepper in large bowl until combined. Add rice, crabmeat, shrimp, scallops and pimientos; toss well.

3. Transfer mixture to prepared casserole; sprinkle with parsley. Cover; bake about 25 minutes or until shrimp and scallops are opaque. *Makes 6 servings*

Salmon Linguini Supper

8 ounces linguini, cooked in unsalted water and drained
1 package (10 ounces) frozen peas
1 cup milk
1 can (10¾ ounces) condensed cream of celery soup
¼ cup (1 ounce) grated Parmesan cheese
⅛ teaspoon dried tarragon, crumbled (optional)
1 can (15½ ounces) salmon, drained and flaked
1 egg, slightly beaten
¼ teaspoon salt
¼ teaspoon pepper
1⅓ cups *French's*® French Fried Onions, divided

Preheat oven to 375°F. Return hot pasta to saucepan; stir in peas, milk, soup, cheese and tarragon; spoon into 12×8-inch baking dish. In medium bowl, using fork, combine salmon, egg, salt, pepper and ⅔ cup French Fried Onions. Shape salmon mixture into 4 oval patties. Place patties on pasta mixture. Bake, covered, at 375°F for 40 minutes or until patties are done. Top patties with remaining ⅔ cup onions; bake, uncovered, 3 minutes or until onions are golden brown.   *Makes 4 servings*

Microwave Directions: Prepare pasta mixture as above, except increase milk to 1¼ cups; spoon into 12×8-inch microwave-safe dish. Cook, covered, on HIGH 3 minutes; stir. Prepare salmon patties as above using 2 eggs. Place patties on pasta mixture. Cook, covered, 10 to 12 minutes or until patties are done. Rotate dish halfway through cooking time. Top patties with remaining onions; cook, uncovered, 1 minute. Let stand 5 minutes.

Broccoli-Fish Roll-Ups

1 can (10¾ ounces) condensed cream of broccoli soup, undiluted
½ cup fat-free (skim) milk
2 cups seasoned stuffing crumbs
¾ pound flounder (4 medium pieces)
1 box (10 ounces) broccoli spears, thawed
Paprika

1. Preheat oven to 375°F. Grease 9×9-inch baking pan. Combine soup and milk in medium bowl. Set aside ½ cup soup mixture.

2. Combine stuffing crumbs and remaining soup mixture. Pat into prepared pan.

3. Place fish on clean work surface. Arrange 1 broccoli spear across narrow end of fish. Starting at narrow end, gently roll up fish. Place over stuffing mixture, seam side down. Repeat with remaining fish and broccoli.

4. Arrange any remaining broccoli spears over stuffing mixture. Spoon reserved ½ cup soup mixture over broccoli-fish roll-ups. Sprinkle with paprika.

5. Bake 20 minutes or until fish flakes easily when tested with fork.

Makes 4 servings

Variation: Asparagus spears and cream of asparagus soup can be substituted for broccoli spears and cream of broccoli soup.

Prep and Cook Time: 30 minutes

Broccoli-Fish Roll-ups

Spicy Crabmeat Frittata

1 tablespoon olive oil
1 medium green bell pepper, finely chopped
2 cloves garlic, minced
6 eggs
1 can (6½ ounces) lump white crabmeat, drained
¼ teaspoon black pepper
¼ teaspoon salt
¼ teaspoon hot pepper sauce
1 large ripe plum tomato, seeded and finely chopped

1. Preheat broiler. Heat oil in 10-inch nonstick skillet with ovenproof handle over medium-high heat. Add bell pepper and garlic; cook and stir 3 minutes or until soft.

2. Meanwhile, beat eggs in medium bowl. Break up large pieces of crabmeat. Add crabmeat, black pepper, salt and pepper sauce to eggs; blend well. Set aside.

3. Add tomato to skillet; cook and stir 1 minute. Add egg mixture. Reduce heat to medium-low; cook about 7 minutes or until eggs begin to set around edges.

4. Remove pan from burner and place under broiler 6 inches from heat. Broil about 2 minutes or until frittata is set and top is browned. Remove from broiler; slide frittata onto serving plate. Serve immediately. *Makes 4 servings*

Tip: Serve with crusty bread, cut-up raw vegetables and guacamole.

Cut the time: Use bottled minced garlic.

Prep & Cook Time: 20 minutes

Spicy Crabmeat Frittata

Baked Fish with Potatoes and Onions

1 pound baking potatoes, very thinly sliced
1 large onion, very thinly sliced
1 small red or green bell pepper, thinly sliced
  Salt
  Black pepper
½ teaspoon dried oregano leaves
  1 pound lean fish fillets, cut 1 inch thick
¼ cup butter or margarine
¼ cup all-purpose flour
  2 cups milk
¾ cup (3 ounces) shredded Cheddar cheese

Preheat oven to 375°F.

Arrange half of potatoes in buttered 3-quart casserole. Top with half of onion and half of bell pepper. Season with salt and black pepper. Sprinkle with half of oregano. Arrange fish in one layer over vegetables. Arrange remaining potatoes, onion and bell pepper over fish. Season with salt, black pepper and remaining oregano.

Melt butter in medium saucepan over medium heat. Stir in flour; cook until bubbly, stirring constantly. Gradually stir in milk. Cook until thickened, stirring constantly. Pour white sauce over casserole. Cover; bake 40 minutes or until potatoes are tender. Sprinkle with cheese. Bake, uncovered, about 5 minutes or until cheese is melted.

Makes 4 servings

Baked Fish with Potatoes and Onions

Crab and Corn Enchilada Casserole

3 cups spicy tomato sauce, divided
10 to 12 ounces fresh crabmeat or flaked or chopped surimi crab
1 package (10 ounces) frozen corn, thawed and drained
1½ cups (6 ounces) shredded reduced-fat Monterey Jack cheese, divided
1 can (4 ounces) diced mild green chilies
12 (6-inch) corn tortillas
1 lime, cut into 6 wedges
Sour cream (optional)

Preheat oven to 350°F. Combine 2 cups spicy tomato sauce, crabmeat, corn, 1 cup cheese and chilies in medium bowl. Cut each tortilla into 4 wedges. Place one-third of tortilla wedges in bottom of shallow 3- to 4-quart casserole, overlapping to make solid layer. Spread half of crab mixture on top. Repeat with another layer of tortilla wedges, remaining crab mixture and remaining tortillas. Spread remaining 1 cup spicy tomato sauce over top; cover.

Bake 30 to 40 minutes or until heated through. Sprinkle with remaining ½ cup cheese; bake uncovered 5 minutes or until cheese melts. Squeeze lime over individual servings. Serve with sour cream, if desired. *Makes 6 servings*

Crab and Corn Enchilada Casserole

Tuna and Broccoli Bake

1 package (16 ounces) frozen broccoli cuts, thawed and well drained
2 slices bread, cut in ½-inch cubes
1 (7-ounce) pouch of STARKIST Flavor Fresh Pouch® Albacore or Chunk Light Tuna
2 cups cottage cheese
1 cup shredded Cheddar cheese
3 eggs
¼ teaspoon ground black pepper

Place broccoli on bottom of 2-quart baking dish. Top with bread cubes and tuna. In medium bowl, combine cottage cheese, Cheddar cheese, eggs and pepper. Spread evenly over tuna mixture. Bake in 400°F oven 30 minutes or until golden brown and puffed. *Makes 4 servings*

Prep Time: 35 minutes

Tuna and Broccoli Bake

Caribbean Shrimp with Rice

1 package (12 ounces) frozen shrimp, thawed
½ cup fat-free reduced-sodium chicken broth
1 clove garlic, minced
1 teaspoon chili powder
½ teaspoon salt
½ teaspoon dried oregano leaves
1 cup frozen peas, thawed
½ cup diced tomatoes
2 cups cooked long-grain white rice

Slow Cooker Directions

1. Combine shrimp, broth, garlic, chili powder, salt and oregano in slow cooker. Cover; cook on LOW 2 hours.

2. Add peas and tomatoes. Cover; cook on LOW 15 minutes.

3. Stir in rice. Cover; cook on LOW an additional 30 minutes.

Makes 4 servings

Florida Grapefruit Marinated Shrimp

1 cup frozen Florida grapefruit juice concentrate, thawed
2 cloves garlic, minced
3 tablespoons chopped fresh cilantro or parsley
1 tablespoon honey
2 teaspoons ketchup
½ teaspoon salt
¼ teaspoon crushed red pepper flakes
1 pound medium raw shrimp, shelled and deveined
2 teaspoons cornstarch
1 cup uncooked long-grain white rice
1 tablespoon olive oil
1 large red bell pepper, cut into strips
2 ribs celery, sliced diagonally into ¼-inch-thick slices
2 Florida grapefruit, peeled and sectioned
Fresh cilantro sprigs

Combine grapefruit juice concentrate, garlic, cilantro, honey, ketchup, salt and red pepper flakes in medium bowl. Stir in shrimp. Marinate 20 minutes, turning shrimp once. Drain shrimp, reserving marinade. Combine marinade with cornstarch. Meanwhile, prepare rice according to package directions. Heat oil over medium-high heat in large nonstick skillet; add shrimp. Cook and stir 2 to 3 minutes until shrimp turn pink and opaque. Add red bell pepper, celery and reserved marinade. Bring to a boil over high heat; boil until mixture thickens slightly, stirring constantly. Add grapefruit and heat 30 seconds. Garnish with fresh sprigs of cilantro.

Makes 4 servings

Favorite recipe from **Florida Department of Citrus**

Shrimp Primavera Pot Pie

1 can (10¾ ounces) condensed cream of shrimp soup, undiluted
1 package (12 ounces) frozen peeled uncooked medium shrimp
2 packages (1 pound each) frozen mixed vegetables, such as green
**   beans, potatoes, onions and red peppers, thawed and drained**
1 teaspoon dried dill weed
¼ teaspoon salt
¼ teaspoon black pepper
1 can (11 ounces) refrigerated breadstick dough

1. Preheat oven to 400°F. Heat soup in medium ovenproof skillet over medium-high heat 1 minute. Add shrimp; cook and stir 3 minutes or until shrimp begin to thaw. Stir in vegetables, dill, salt and pepper; mix well. Reduce heat to medium-low; cook and stir 3 minutes.

2. Unwrap breadstick dough; separate into 8 strips. Twist strips, cutting to fit skillet. Arrange attractively over shrimp mixture in crisscross pattern. Press ends of dough lightly to edges of skillet to secure. Bake 18 minutes or until crust is golden brown and shrimp mixture is bubbly.   *Makes 4 to 6 servings*

Prep and Cook Time: 30 minutes

Shrimp Primavera Pot Pie

Shrimp Creole

2 tablespoons olive oil
1½ cups chopped green bell pepper
1 medium onion, chopped
⅔ cup chopped celery
2 cloves garlic, finely chopped
1 cup uncooked long-grain rice
1 can (about 14 ounces) diced tomatoes, drained and juice reserved
1 teaspoon dried oregano leaves
¾ teaspoon salt
½ teaspoon dried thyme leaves
2 teaspoons hot pepper sauce, or to taste
Black pepper
1 pound raw shrimp, peeled and deveined
1 tablespoon chopped fresh parsley (optional)

1. Preheat oven to 325°F. Heat olive oil in large skillet over medium-high heat. Add bell pepper, onion, celery and garlic; cook and stir 5 minutes or until vegetables are soft.

2. Add rice; cook and stir 5 minutes over medium heat until rice is opaque. Add tomatoes, oregano, salt, thyme, hot sauce and black pepper to skillet; cook and stir to combine. Pour reserved tomato juice into measuring cup. Add enough water to measure 1¾ cups liquid; add to skillet. Cook and stir 2 minutes.

3. Transfer mixture to 2½-quart casserole. Stir in shrimp. Bake, covered, 55 minutes or until rice is tender and liquid is absorbed. Sprinkle with parsley, if desired.

Makes 4 to 6 servings

Shrimp Creole

Lickety-Split Paella Pronto

1 tablespoon olive oil
1 large onion, chopped
2 cloves garlic, minced
1 jar (16 ounces) salsa
1 can (14½ ounces) diced tomatoes, undrained
1 can (14 ounces) artichoke hearts, drained and quartered
1 can (14 ounces) chicken broth
1 package (about 8 ounces) uncooked yellow rice
1 can (12 ounces) solid white tuna, drained and flaked
1 package (9 to 10 ounces) frozen green peas
2 tablespoons finely chopped green onions (optional)
2 tablespoons finely chopped red bell pepper (optional)

1. Heat oil in large nonstick skillet over medium heat until hot. Add onion and garlic; cook and stir about 5 minutes or until onion is tender.

2. Stir in salsa, tomatoes with juice, artichokes, broth and rice. Bring to a boil. Cover; reduce heat to low and simmer 15 minutes.

3. Stir in tuna and peas. Cover; cook 5 to 10 minutes or until rice is tender and tuna and peas are heated through. Sprinkle each serving with green onions and red bell pepper, if desired. *Makes 4 to 6 servings*

Lickety-Split Paella Pronto

Mom's Tuna Casserole

2 cans (12 ounces each) tuna, drained and flaked
3 cups diced celery
3 cups crushed potato chips, divided
6 hard-cooked eggs, chopped
1 can (10¾ ounces) condensed cream of mushroom soup, undiluted
1 can (10¾ ounces) condensed cream of celery soup, undiluted
1 cup mayonnaise
1 teaspoon dried tarragon leaves
1 teaspoon ground black pepper

Slow Cooker Directions

1. Combine tuna, celery, 2½ cups potato chips, eggs, soups, mayonnaise, tarragon and pepper in slow cooker; stir well.

2. Sprinkle with remaining ½ cup potato chips.

3. Cover; cook on LOW 5 to 8 hours.   *Makes 8 servings*

Mom's Tuna Casserole

Creamy "Crab" Fettuccine

1 pound imitation crabmeat sticks
6 ounces uncooked fettuccine
3 tablespoons margarine or butter, divided
1 small onion, chopped
2 ribs celery, chopped
½ medium red bell pepper, chopped
2 cloves garlic, minced
1 cup reduced-fat sour cream
1 cup reduced-fat mayonnaise
1 cup (4 ounces) shredded sharp Cheddar cheese
2 tablespoons chopped fresh parsley
¼ teaspoon salt
⅛ teaspoon black pepper
½ cup cornflake crumbs
Fresh chives (optional)

1. Preheat oven to 350°F. Spray 2-quart square baking dish with nonstick cooking spray. Cut crabmeat into bite-size pieces. Cook pasta according to package directions until al dente. Drain and set aside.

2. Meanwhile, melt 1 tablespoon margarine in large skillet over medium-high heat. Add onion, celery, bell pepper and garlic; cook and stir 2 minutes or until vegetables are tender.

3. Combine sour cream, mayonnaise, cheese, parsley, salt and black pepper in large bowl. Add crabmeat, pasta and vegetable mixture, stirring gently to combine. Pour into prepared dish.

4. Melt remaining 2 tablespoons margarine. Combine cornflake crumbs and margarine in small bowl; sprinkle evenly over casserole.

5. Bake, uncovered, 30 minutes or until hot and bubbly. Garnish with chives, if desired.

Makes 6 servings

Creamy "Crab" Fettuccine

Slow-Simmered Jambalaya

2 cans (14½ ounces each) stewed tomatoes, undrained
2 cups diced boiled ham
2 medium onions, coarsely chopped
1 medium green bell pepper, diced
2 ribs celery, sliced
1 cup uncooked long-grain converted rice
2 tablespoons vegetable oil
2 tablespoons ketchup
3 cloves garlic, minced
½ teaspoon dried thyme leaves
½ teaspoon black pepper
⅛ teaspoon ground cloves
1 pound fresh or frozen raw shrimp, peeled and deveined

Slow Cooker Directions

1. Thoroughly mix tomatoes, ham, onions, bell pepper, celery, rice, oil, ketchup, garlic, thyme, black pepper and cloves in slow cooker.

2. Cover; cook on LOW 8 to 10 hours.

3. One hour before serving, turn slow cooker to HIGH. Stir in shrimp. Cover; cook until shrimp are pink and tender.   *Makes 4 to 6 servings*

Creole Shrimp and Rice

2 tablespoons olive oil
1 cup uncooked white rice
1 can (15 ounces) diced tomatoes with garlic, undrained
1½ cups water
1 teaspoon Creole or Cajun seasoning blend
1 pound peeled cooked medium shrimp
**1 package (10 ounces) frozen okra *or* 1½ cups frozen sugar snap
    peas, thawed**

1. Heat oil in large skillet over medium heat until hot. Add rice; cook and
stir 2 to 3 minutes or until lightly browned.

2. Add tomatoes with juice, water and seasoning blend; bring to a boil. Reduce
heat; cover and simmer 15 minutes.

3. Add shrimp and okra. Cook, covered, 3 minutes or until heated through.

Makes 4 servings

Note: Okra are oblong green pods. When cooked, it gives off a viscous substance
that acts as a good thickener for soups and stews.

Prep and Cook Time: 20 minutes

Seafood Lasagna

1 package (16 ounces) lasagna noodles
2 tablespoons margarine or butter
1 large onion, finely chopped
1 package (8 ounces) cream cheese, cut into ½-inch pieces, softened
1½ cups cream-style cottage cheese
2 teaspoons dried basil leaves
½ teaspoon salt
⅛ teaspoon black pepper
1 egg, lightly beaten
2 cans (10¾ ounces each) condensed cream of mushroom soup, undiluted
⅓ cup milk
1 clove garlic, minced
½ pound bay scallops, rinsed and patted dry
½ pound flounder fillets, rinsed, patted dry and cut into ½-inch cubes
½ pound medium raw shrimp, peeled and deveined
½ cup dry white wine
1 cup (4 ounces) shredded mozzarella cheese
2 tablespoons grated Parmesan cheese

1. Cook lasagna noodles according to package directions; drain.

2. Melt margarine in large skillet over medium heat. Cook onion in hot margarine until tender, stirring frequently. Stir in cream cheese, cottage cheese, basil, salt and pepper; mix well. Stir in egg; set aside.

3. Combine soup, milk and garlic in large bowl until well blended. Stir in scallops, fish fillets, shrimp and wine.

4. Preheat oven to 350°F. Grease 13×9-inch baking pan.

5. Place layer of noodles in prepared pan, overlapping noodles. Spread half the cheese mixture over noodles. Place layer of noodles over cheese mixture and top with half the seafood mixture. Repeat layers. Sprinkle with mozzarella and Parmesan cheeses.

6. Bake 45 minutes or until bubbly. Let stand 10 minutes before cutting.

Makes 8 to 10 servings

Seafood Lasagna

Tuna in Squash Shells

4 medium zucchini, yellow zucchini or yellow crookneck squash
¼ cup diced carrot
¼ cup chopped green onions
2 tablespoons bottled reduced-calorie Italian dressing
1 (7-ounce) pouch of STARKIST Flavor Fresh Pouch® Albacore or Chunk Light Tuna
¼ cup cooked white or brown rice
¼ teaspoon garlic powder
¼ teaspoon pepper
½ cup shredded low-fat Cheddar, Swiss or mozzarella cheese

Cut squash lengthwise into halves. Trim a very thin slice from bottom of each squash half so it will sit upright. Scoop out the pulp from each squash half, leaving ¼-inch-thick shells. Chop the pulp; set aside. Place squash shells in boiling water to cover for 5 minutes. Rinse in cold water. Drain shells well, upside down, on paper towels. Set aside.

Preheat oven to 375°F. For filling, in a skillet sauté carrot, onions and chopped squash pulp in Italian dressing for 3 minutes. Stir in tuna, rice and seasonings until well combined. Mound filling mixture in shells. Spray a shallow baking dish with nonstick cooking spray. Place shells in dish; cover with foil. Bake for 20 minutes. Uncover; top with cheese. Bake for 5 minutes more, or until heated through.

Makes 4 servings

Prep Time: 25 minutes

Tuna in Squash Shells

Salmon Casserole

    2 tablespoons butter or margarine
    2 cups mushroom slices
1½ cups chopped carrots
    1 cup frozen peas
    1 cup chopped celery
 ½ cup chopped onion
 ½ cup chopped red bell pepper
    1 tablespoon chopped fresh parsley
    1 clove garlic, minced
    1 teaspoon salt
 ½ teaspoon black pepper
 ½ teaspoon dried basil leaves
    4 cups cooked rice
    1 can (14 ounces) red salmon, drained and flaked
    1 can (10¾ ounces) condensed cream of mushroom soup, undiluted
    2 cups (8 ounces) grated Cheddar or American cheese
 ½ cup sliced black olives

1. Preheat oven to 350°F. Spray 2-quart casserole with nonstick cooking spray; set aside.

2. Melt butter in large skillet or Dutch oven over medium heat. Add mushrooms, carrots, peas, celery, onion, bell pepper, parsley, garlic, salt, black pepper and basil; cook and stir 10 minutes or until vegetables are tender. Add rice, salmon, soup and cheese; mix well.

3. Transfer to prepared casserole. Sprinkle olives over top. Bake 30 minutes or until hot and bubbly.   *Makes 8 servings*

Salmon Casserole

Crab-Artichoke Casserole

8 ounces uncooked small shell pasta
2 tablespoons butter
6 green onions, chopped
2 tablespoons all-purpose flour
1 cup half-and-half
1 teaspoon dry mustard
½ teaspoon ground red pepper
    Salt and black pepper
½ cup (2 ounces) shredded Swiss cheese, divided
1 package (about 8 ounces) imitation crabmeat chunks
1 can (about 14 ounces) artichoke hearts, drained and cut into
    bite-size pieces

1. Preheat oven to 350°F. Grease 2-quart casserole. Cook pasta according to package directions; drain and set aside.

2. Heat butter in large saucepan over medium heat; add green onions. Cook and stir about 2 minutes. Add flour; cook and stir 2 minutes more. Gradually add half-and-half, whisking constantly until mixture begins to thicken. Whisk in mustard and red pepper; season to taste with salt and black pepper. Remove from heat and stir in ¼ cup cheese until melted.

3. Combine crabmeat, artichokes and pasta in casserole. Add sauce mixture and stir well. Top with remaining ¼ cup cheese. Bake about 40 minutes or until hot, bubbly and lightly browned. *Makes 6 servings*

Tip: This can also be baked in individual ovenproof dishes. Reduce cooking time to about 20 minutes.

Crab-Artichoke Casserole

Impossibly Easy Salmon Pie

1 can (7½ ounces) salmon packed in water, drained and deboned
½ cup grated Parmesan cheese
¼ cup sliced green onions
1 jar (2 ounces) chopped pimientos, drained
½ cup low-fat (1%) cottage cheese
1 tablespoon lemon juice
1½ cups low-fat (1%) milk
¾ cup reduced-fat baking and pancake mix
2 whole eggs
2 egg whites *or* ¼ cup cholesterol-free egg substitute
¼ teaspoon salt
¼ teaspoon dried dill weed
¼ teaspoon paprika (optional)

1. Preheat oven to 375°F. Spray 9-inch pie plate with nonstick cooking spray. Combine salmon, Parmesan cheese, onions and pimientos in prepared pie plate; set aside.

2. Combine cottage cheese and lemon juice in blender or food processor; blend until smooth. Add milk, baking mix, whole eggs, egg whites, salt and dill. Blend 15 seconds. Pour over salmon mixture in pie plate. Sprinkle with paprika, if desired.

3. Bake 35 to 40 minutes or until lightly golden and knife inserted halfway between center and edge comes out clean. Cool 5 minutes. Cut into 8 wedges before serving. Garnish as desired.

Makes 8 servings

Impossibly Easy Salmon Pie

Acknowledgments

The publisher would like to thank the companies and organizations listed below for the use of their recipes and photographs in this publication.

Birds Eye® Foods

Del Monte Corporation

Filippo Berio® Olive Oil

Florida Department of Agriculture and Consumer Services, Bureau of Seafood and Aquaculture

Florida's Citrus Growers

The Golden Grain Company®

The Hidden Valley® Food Products Company

Hillshire Farm®

MASTERFOODS USA

National Onion Association

Reckitt Benckiser Inc.

Sargento® Foods Inc.

StarKist Seafood Company

Unilever Foods North America

USA Rice Federation

Veg•All®

Index

A

Ale'd Pork and Sauerkraut, 190

Apple
Chicken Normandy Style, 148
Pork Chops and Apple Stuffing Bake, 152
Pork with Savory Apple Stuffing, 168
Simply Delicious Pork, 190
Sweet Kraut Chops, 158

Artichokes
Artichoke-Olive Chicken Bake, 132
Crab-Artichoke Casserole, 306
Lickety-Split Paella Pronto, 292
Vegetarian Paella, 232

Asparagus: Baked Risotto with Asparagus, Spinach & Parmesan, 220

Autumn Delight, 72

B

Baked Fish with Potatoes and Onions, 280

Baked Risotto with Asparagus, Spinach & Parmesan, 220

Barbecue Sauce
Barbecued Pulled Pork, 184
Chuckwagon BBQ Rice Round-Up, 46
Shredded Apricot Pork Sandwiches, 178
Sweet & Saucy Ribs, 198
Sweet 'n' Spicy Ribs, 162

Barley: Cheesy Baked Barley, 228

Bayou-Style Pot Pie, 144

Beans
Beef & Bean Burritos, 52
Beef Picante and Sour Cream Casserole, 82
Cannellini Parmesan Casserole, 213

Beans *(continued)*
Carolina Baked Beans & Pork Chops, 164
Chili with Beans and Corn, 204
Easy Moroccan Casserole, 156
Fiery Chili Beef, 34
Indian Vegetable Curry, 244
Layered Mexican Tortilla Cheese Casserole, 230
Mediterranean Stew, 208
Mexican Skillet Rice, 192
Mile-High Enchilada Pie, 106
Moroccan Supper, 240
Quick Veg•All® Enchiladas, 233
Spinach and Mushroom Enchiladas, 225
Vegetarian Paella, 232
Vegetarian Sausage Rice, 250

Beef & Bean Burritos, 52

Beef & Broccoli Pepper Steak, 30

Beef (34-91): Old-Fashioned Cabbage Rolls, 166

Beef and Parsnip Stroganoff, 64

Beef and Vegetables in Rich Burgundy Sauce, 40

Beef Bourguignon, 66

Beef in Wine Sauce, 84

Beef Picante and Sour Cream Casserole, 82

Beef Roll-Ups, 79

Biscuit-Topped Hearty Steak Pie, 74

Braciola, 54

Bread Crumbs
Broccoli & Cheddar Noodle Casserole, 210
Broccoli-Fish Roll-Ups, 276
Eggplant Parmigiana, 202
Escalloped Chicken, 104
Old-Fashioned Cabbage Rolls, 166

Bread Crumbs *(continued)*
Pasta with Salmon and Dill, 266
Pizza Pie Meatloaf, 42
Pork Meatballs & Sauerkraut, 188
Slow Cooker Meatloaf, 79

Broccoli
Beef & Broccoli Pepper Steak, 30
Broccoli & Cheese Strata, 218
Broccoli & Cheddar Noodle Casserole, 210
Broccoli, Chicken and Rice Casserole, 102
Broccoli-Fish Roll-Ups, 276
Easy Chicken Alfredo, 142
Farmstand Frittata, 212
Fish Broccoli Casserole, 274
Flounder Fillets over Zesty Lemon Rice, 262
Herb-Baked Fish & Rice, 268
Moroccan Supper, 240
Shredded Pork Wraps, 160
Tomato, Basil & Broccoli Chicken, 131
Tuna and Broccoli Bake, 284

Broccoli & Cheese Strata, 218

Broccoli & Cheddar Noodle Casserole, 210

Broccoli, Chicken and Rice Casserole, 102

Broccoli-Fish Roll-Ups, 276

C

Cabbage
Corned Beef and Cabbage, 80
Old-Fashioned Cabbage Rolls, 166

Cajun-Style Country Ribs, 154

Cannellini Parmesan Casserole, 213

Cantonese Pork, 186

METRIC CONVERSION CHART

VOLUME MEASUREMENTS (dry)

¹/₈ teaspoon = 0.5 mL
¹/₄ teaspoon = 1 mL
¹/₂ teaspoon = 2 mL
³/₄ teaspoon = 4 mL
1 teaspoon = 5 mL
1 tablespoon = 15 mL
2 tablespoons = 30 mL
¹/₄ cup = 60 mL
¹/₃ cup = 75 mL
¹/₂ cup = 125 mL
²/₃ cup = 150 mL
³/₄ cup = 175 mL
1 cup = 250 mL
2 cups = 1 pint = 500 mL
3 cups = 750 mL
4 cups = 1 quart = 1 L

VOLUME MEASUREMENTS (fluid)

1 fluid ounce (2 tablespoons) = 30 mL
4 fluid ounces (¹/₂ cup) = 125 mL
8 fluid ounces (1 cup) = 250 mL
12 fluid ounces (1¹/₂ cups) = 375 mL
16 fluid ounces (2 cups) = 500 mL

WEIGHTS (mass)

¹/₂ ounce = 15 g
1 ounce = 30 g
3 ounces = 90 g
4 ounces = 120 g
8 ounces = 225 g
10 ounces = 285 g
12 ounces = 360 g
16 ounces = 1 pound = 450 g

DIMENSIONS

¹/₁₆ inch = 2 mm
¹/₈ inch = 3 mm
¹/₄ inch = 6 mm
¹/₂ inch = 1.5 cm
³/₄ inch = 2 cm
1 inch = 2.5 cm

OVEN TEMPERATURES

250°F = 120°C
275°F = 140°C
300°F = 150°C
325°F = 160°C
350°F = 180°C
375°F = 190°C
400°F = 200°C
425°F = 220°C
450°F = 230°C

BAKING PAN SIZES

Utensil	Size in Inches/Quarts	Metric Volume	Size in Centimeters
Baking or Cake Pan (square or rectangular)	8×8×2	2 L	20×20×5
	9×9×2	2.5 L	23×23×5
	12×8×2	3 L	30×20×5
	13×9×2	3.5 L	33×23×5
Loaf Pan	8×4×3	1.5 L	20×10×7
	9×5×3	2 L	23×13×7
Round Layer Cake Pan	8×1½	1.2 L	20×4
	9×1½	1.5 L	23×4
Pie Plate	8×1¼	750 mL	20×3
	9×1¼	1 L	23×3
Baking Dish or Casserole	1 quart	1 L	—
	1½ quart	1.5 L	—
	2 quart	2 L	—